The Muslim's handbook to understanding China

Compilation of Question & Answers issued by Hizb ut Tahrir & its Ameer, the eminent scholar Shekh Ata bin Khalil Abu Rashta

istinarah Press

Istinarah Press

MaktabaIslamia Publications

www.maktabaislamia.com
info@maktabaislamia.com
www.facebook.com/everythingislamic
www.twitter.com/maktabaislamia

2016 CE – 1437 H

Translation of the Qur'ān

It should be perfectly clear that the Qur'ān is only authentic in its original language, Arabic. Since perfect translation of the Qur'ān is impossible, we have used the translation of the meaning of the Qur'ān throughout the book, as the result is only a crude meaning of the Arabic text.

Qur'ānic verses appear in speech marks proceeded by a reference to the Surah and verse number. Sayings (*Hadith*) of Prophet Muhammad ﷺ appear in inverted commas along with reference to the Hadith Book and its Reporter.

ﷺ - (صلى الله عليه وسلم)(Peace be upon him)

ﷻ - (سبحانه وتعالى)(Glory to Him, the Exalted)

Contents

Publishers Forward

This book has been written as a result of a need to have a handy guide to understand various Intellectual, Economic, Legislative & Political issues from an Islamic ideological perspective.

As time progresses and with the ever increasing call among the Muslims to reunite under a Khilafah where Islamic is implemented in a comprehensive manner, there is an increasing need for books to be written on crucial subjects so as to be able to build within the Ummah the right awareness and depth.

Having felt the need, we have embarked on this ambitious project to produce books on subjects that are pertinent to the Ummahs culturing, subjects that have not yet been brought out in the form of books.

The 'Muslim ideologue's Companion' series is a unique series that Team Maktaba has worked to compile and bring forth addressing a range of subjects including indepth studies & analysis on regional and international powers, important economic issues such as Oil pricing and the Global Economic Crisis & Legislative opinions on the working of the very soon to be established Khilafah Rashidah.

Most of our content has been compiled from existing articles, books & Question and Answers answered by the Shekh Ata bin Khaleel abu Rashta, the current Ameer of the world's largest Islamic political party, Hizb ut Tahrir and other authors and writers on the subjects.

Chapter 1

An Introduction to China

China: Past & Present

China: Pretender or Contender

Today it has become difficult to not notice the rise of China. China is now the world's largest economy after the US, it has also replaced Germany as the world's largest exporter and it now even consumes more Saudi oil then the USA. In the last decade many analysts have viewed the rise of China as America's biggest challenge and some thinkers foresee China as the world's superpower in the not so distant future. The rapid rise of China on the global map in the last 30 years has shocked many, bewildered others and for some marks the shift of global power from West to East. Some have even touted a new model for economic development called the 'the China Model.'

Historically nations gained strength through the efficient harnessing of mineral resources, through economic development, through constructing a military that could defend the nation and expand the nation's foreign policy goals and ideology. All of these were usually driven by global aims of spreading the nation's culture or way of life. This article will trace how China managed to change its situation and asses if China really is in a position to pose a challenge to the US and shift the global balance of power.

Understanding Chinese Development

China as a nation has existed for over 4000 years. Most of Chinese history consists of internal struggles between various dynasties fighting to rule over the nation. Modern China emerged after WW2 when the Japanese who occupied large parts of China were defeated. The resultant vacuum led to civil war between the Chinese nationalists supported by the West and Chinese communists led by Mao Zedong, who was supported by the Soviet Union.

Mao and his communists defeated the nationalists and then ruled China with Communism for the next 3 decades. The Communists launched 2 disastrous strategies to develop China, the first of them – the great leap forward in 1953, attempted to collectivize all aspects of life (even cooking pots), this strategy led to a famine and the death of 30 million people. This disaster of epic proportions gave birth to the reform movement in China which has been central to China's rapid economic development.

Mao then initiated the Cultural Revolution in 1966 in order to do away with such undesirables, Mao believed, in accordance with permanent revolution, that such elements should be removed through revolutionary violence, leading to another period of instability in China's long and turbulent history.

The death of Mao in 1976 led to the emergence of the reformists and chief architect of China's current economic development - Deng Xiaoping. Under his leadership an analysis of the nation was undertaken by technocrats from the Chinese Communist Party and published in three documents called the Four Modernizations. The analysis concluded that the prior efforts to develop China, had been failures. It proposed a new comprehensive policy for China, based on a number of underpinnings. The most important of these were the following:

Firstly, the realization that China possessed many of strengths needed to become a global superpower. It had the agrarian land to be self sufficient in its food supply. The sheer size of China's population gives it the ability to become economically independent i.e. the Chinese market is so big that every local demand – both civilian and military could efficiently be produced domestically. If managed properly, such strengths combined could give China the financial ability to develop its armed forces. Through which the country could then become an all-round global superpower.

Secondly, the realization that China would never achieve its potential if it did not increase its knowledge base. If China ever wanted to challenge the then foremost powers of the day, America and the Soviet-Union, the Chinese workforce would need to make 'great leaps forward' in both technical and managerial knowledge.

Thirdly, the realization that its population, and in particular the growth of its population, could become the nation's Achilles heal. If Chinese population growth was not matched with economic growth and employment then the resulting mass unemployment would cause mass poverty, civil unrest and a revolt against the rule of the Communist Party.

The reformists view was that developing China economically was not just an aspiration but a necessity. This comprehensive analysis of China's state of affairs was translated into policy in 1979 and saw the birth of China's 'open door' economic policy that led to rapid economic development. China's 'open door' economic policy gradually opened up China's economy to foreign companies through the establishment of Special Economic Zones (SEZs), in a process well controlled by the Communist Party. However this was not simply an exercise in economic growth, the real aim was much broader.

The use of Foreign Direct Investment (FDI), although greatly aided economic activity and job creation, it also allowed for foreign technical and managerial knowledge into China. This is why to this day all foreign companies in China are forced to transfer technical knowledge. The 2010 US-China Economic and Security Review Commission, which advises the US Congress on China related policy issues, confirmed this, regarding China's strategies for developing its aviation industrial base it said: *'Beijing's strategies include the government's heavy political and fiscal support for China's aviation manufacturing industry and the requirement for foreign aviation firms to provide technology and know-how offsets in return for market access'.*

The explanation by many that China's rapid economic success was due to opening up to Capitalism is not correct. What really took place was China, after a careful review of its strengths and weaknesses, developed an economic policy that enabled it to benefit from its economic strengths and at the same time address its economic weaknesses.

China - US relations

US policy makers spelled out their strategy for China initially in the Defence Planning Guidance (DPG) for fiscal years 1994-99, the first formal statement of US strategic goals in the post-Soviet era, it stated: *"we [must] endeavour to prevent any hostile power from dominating a region whose resources would, under consolidated control, be sufficient to generate global power."*

By the time George W Bush came to office only China possessed the economic and military capacity to challenge the United States as an aspiring superpower. The US developed a policy of containment rather than outright competition with China in order to restrain it within its borders ensuring no-one shares the Asia Pacific with her. This policy of containment was spelt out by Condoleezza Rice while serving as a foreign-policy adviser to George W Bush, then governor of the state of Texas, during the 2000 presidential campaign in a Foreign Affairs article she stated *"China is a great power with unresolved vital interests, particularly concerning Taiwan, China also resents the role of the United States in the Asia-Pacific region."*

For these reasons, she stated, *"China is not a 'status quo' power but one that would like to alter Asia's balance of power in its own favour. That alone makes it a strategic competitor, not the 'strategic partner' the Clinton administration once called it. The United States must deepen its cooperation with Japan and South Korea and maintain its commitment to a robust military presence in the region"*. Washington should *also "pay closer attention to India's role in the regional balance, and bring that country into an anti-Chinese alliance system."*

To achieve this America has upgraded security relations with Japan and has supported Japanese calls for nuclear development. This would mean abandoning the decades old constitutional defensive policy. On the Western flank India has been wooed with economic deals, the transfer of nuclear technology and ambitions of permanent Security Council status. The US in a similar manner has normalised relations with Vietnam burying its historical conflict and forming bilateral partnerships with it. The US has successfully manoeuvred the Vietnamese to increase interaction with it, breaking the age old Chinese links to the pacific region. Vietnam continues to have a territorial dispute on its northern border with China.

The US has also used its conflict with North Korea to contain China. Whilst the US has offered various incentives for Pyongyang to give up its nuclear enrichment programme, the US has never delivered on any of its promises. Whilst China has pursued six party talks with North Korea the statements from such meetings have been contradictory where China has been remarking pessimistic talks with distance on issues to the US remarking successful negotiations. The North and South Korea issue gives a suitable justification for sustained and substantial US presence in South Korea.

The US has also announced in September 2009 a shift in policy towards Myanmar (Burma). It plans to move beyond the current sanctions regime to include direct engagement with the military government. Myanmar is playing a central role in China's overseas energy strategy and through direct engagement the US is attempting to minimise the expansion of a Chinese sphere of influence in Asia.

Washington pushed ahead with its strategy to re-engage with Southeast Asia and to re-assert its commitment to the region's security in the summer of

2010. It engaged in various military exercises to bolster the regions security against China.

China has challenged America's containment policy by using its economic card to loosen US relations with nations in its region. China has through trade developed bilateral ties to loosen US relations with the likes of India, Japan, Indonesia and South Korea. China is also much confident in asserting its right to the South China Sea and declaring its right over a number of islands in the Asia Pacific as the US is viewed by China to be weaker today due to the Afghan and Iraq wars and the global economic crisis.

China Today

Economy - After three decades of phenomenal growth China has become the industrial factory of the world, producing many of the world's consumer items. Domestically, government investment and exports are the twin engines of the economy. In the last decade China has moved 700 million of it citizens out of poverty.

China's growth has come from both huge state investment in infrastructure and heavy industry. 159 large state owned enterprises – these SOEs, provide key inputs from utilities, heavy industries and energy resources that facilitate the private sector. The aggressive outward investment strategy, driven by state-owned enterprises and state banks with massive pools of cash that have allowed China to spread across the world looking to expand markets, employ their services and buy up resources.

Foreign Policy - Economic power has also driven China's foreign policy. Chinese policy makers, officials and scholars describe the country's foreign policy approach as a 'peaceful rise.' China has seeked to characterise itself as a responsible world leader, emphasising soft power, and vowed that it is committed to its own internal issues rather than interfering with global issues. China's foreign policy is centred on domestic economic development and procuring all the necessary raw materials to achieve such aims.

The execution of China's foreign policy represents an important evolution from Beijing's narrow and reactive approach to global affairs in the past. China is abandoning its long-held victim mentality of 150 years of shame and humiliation and adopting instead a great power mentality. The natural extension of this is the increasing role of China in global issues. This has been driven by leading members of the Communist party who were not born during the Chinese revolution and hence do not view the world from the perspective of China's history.

Leaders, such as the current president Hu Jintao, who was born only a few years before the Chinese revolution, was China's first leader not to have taken part in the infamous long march. It is such leaders who believe in the abandonment of China's victim mentality and the adoption of a great power mentality, it is such leaders who are increasingly seeing China more akin to the world's major powers.

As Beijing's economic might has increased so has its influence in its periphery. China is looking to modernise its military and naval capabilities and has become more strident regarding its territorial claims in the South China Sea, a crucial waterway for the US and Japan. China continues to use its economic card to loosen US ties in the region as these countries seek to profit from the extraordinary economic boom in China - fuelled to a considerable extent by oil, gas, iron, timber, and other materials supplied by China's neighbours in Asia.

In Africa China is constructing bridges, dams, roads, railroads and football stadiums, oil refineries in exchange for oil, gas, coal, zinc and copper. Chinese businesses view Africa as Chinese management of Africa's unskilled labour for the continent's vast resources as fire and fuel for China's economic engine. The Chinese leadership characterizes this policy as a principled stance of "non-intervention" in Africa's domestic politics.

Military - At the height of the Cold War, Soviet military vessels prowled the world's oceans, and its aircrafts patrolled international airspace. By contrast, China's navy rarely leaves its home waters; when it does patrol farther afield, it still does not cross the Pacific. China has not stated its aspirations to conquer the globe or establish distant bases. China's military doctrine is built upon minimum deterrence – i.e. having the minimum military capability to ensure it cannot be blackmailed.

Militarily China's has undergone considerable development. Mao's doctrine of 'human wave attacks' - having more soldiers than your enemy has bullets has been replaced with a smaller armed force (relatively) emphasizing new technologies. China's military development has been driven by the need to protect itself in the region and its supply lines. The Chinese military is currently seeking to project naval power well beyond the Chinese coast, from the oil ports of the Middle East to the shipping lanes of the Pacific, where the US has long reigned as the dominant force.

China quantitatively and qualitatively lags behind the US and Russia and much of its military equipment was developed during the Vietnam War. Whilst China is making rapid advances it is still a number of generations away from a military capability that can go beyond its region. China still maintains a reliance on Russian weapons systems and still cannot make reliable engines. In light of its generational deficiencies cyber warfare provides China with an asymmetric advantage to deter aggression from stronger military powers as they catch up in traditional military capabilities.

For China, weapons and technology acquisitions are a high priority as it continues in its attempts to modernize its military, primarily through the purchase and illicit acquisition of foreign technology and subsequently reverse engineering that technology so it can be produced domestically. China has placed an importance on trimming down its size of its armed forces, favouring quality over quantity. China's weaponry often lags one or two generations behind that of Western military powers. However, the total force base still poses a significant deterrent, and establishes China as a dominant power within the Asia-Pacific Region. China lacks force projection beyond its region, primarily due to the lack of a blue water navy and aircraft carrier fleet, but also due to limits in missile technology and air-defence penetration, and opposition by foreign powers such as the US. China seeks to become self-sufficient in many of these key capabilities. If that can be achieved China will no longer need such wide scale technology transfer and could then flex some muscle.

Issues

In China's history it has never been a superpower and has never influenced the global balance of power. Even when it adopted Communism it never carried this beyond its borders and never influenced any of the regions of the world. Much of China's 4000 year history is composed of internal wars and struggles in order to unify the homeland. China's foreign policy is centred on domestic economic development and procuring all the necessary raw materials to achieve such aims. In the decades ahead China faces the following challenges that it will need to address if it wants to be the world super power, these include:

China has undergone some radical changes in the last few decades, however these changes are not due to a transformation of its beliefs, but the confidence and ambition that China should be the dominant power in the region. The ambition driving China is its national interests rather than any ideology. This is different to the US as she possesses a vision that its culture and way of life should be the reference point for the whole world. The main obstacle for Chinese domination is a country that is not even a resident of its neighbourhood. China has not devoted the advancing of any higher international ideological call such as communism or democracy. Ideology appears to be secondary to advancing its national interests. The problem with this is as the country's economy grows the demand for energy resources will continue to grow. This creates a need for solid international relations with exporting nations and the need for securing transportation routes, all of this requires a consistent set of polices.

A decade on however both the US and China have to a large extent become interdependent upon each other. Whilst the US dominated all regions of the world at the turn of the century, Afghanistan and Iraq as well as the global financial crisis has resulted in the US being unable to dominate the relationship. Sino-US interdependency can be seen from the following: The US, the world's largest consumer, imports the vast majority of the goods that come of China's production lines. The US has a trade deficit of $226 billion (2009) with China, as a result US dollars end up in China, which today is over $2 trillion. Such huge reserves have resulted in China purchasing US treasury bonds, which funds America's massive trade deficit. In turn this is resulted in the expansion of China's manufacturing base, China's need for a larger share of the world's oil and mineral resources. This has also led to the loss of jobs in America's manufacturing sector to superior Chinese craftsmanship. Any unilateral move by China will have an impact on its own economy.

Due to this reality China has for the moment focussed on its region and as of yet has shown only tentative signs of ambition translated into policy beyond the region. China's 'string of pearls' policy is its first venture beyond the region. The policy was described by the US government as follows: *"The "String of Pearls" describes the manifestation of China's rising geopolitical influence through efforts to increase access to ports and airfields, develop special diplomatic relationships, and modernize military forces that extend from the South China Sea through the Strait of Malacca, across the Indian Ocean, and on to the Persian*

Gulf." The sea lines run through the strategic choke points as well as other strategic naval interests along Pakistan, Sri Lanka, Maldives and Somalia are all key strategic routes for oil and gas and will inevitably lead to a clash with the US.

China currently has shown little global ambition in constructing an alternative global system. It has in fact amalgamated into America's global system of trade - WTO, security – United Nations and finance – G8 & G20 etc. China appears to be working to achieve its interests from the existing system rather than attempting to replace it. With such a narrow view China will politically never be able to challenge the US.

China's development is rooted in Deng Xiaoping's attempts at creating special economic zones (SEZ) which allowed foreign investment and technology and became a new source of wealth. China today is an export oriented economy and dependent on foreign countries to continue importing from it. Therefore whatever the size of China's currency reserves, no matter how cheap it's labour force or its technological developments, China relies on foreign nations to import from it and physically ship them – A naval blockade would cripple China. The world imports from China at the cost of closing down their own factories, as long as no other nation produces the worlds goods cheaper than China, China will remain the world's workshop. China today is the world's industrial workshop; it remains totally dependent on the world to continue buying from it rather than anyone else, this is a very fragile model of development.

Whilst many have called China's economic model state capitalism, the reality is China has not adhered to any consistent and ideological model of economic development; reform in China was driven by pragmatism and a piecemeal approach to instigating and managing change. China focused on export-oriented growth and gradual liberalization of certain markets combined with an outward looking foreign investment strategy. What China has been very successful at is the rolling out of its polices. All major reforms have been the result of a process of trial and error on a limited scale. Successful experiments are then scaled up and rolled out across the country. Thus the establishment and success of four special economic zones in the 1980s was a crucial precursor to its expansion. How China will deal with the resultant wealth that results form this success remains to be seen when it has no reference point or ideology to refer to.

Being the world's Industrial factory has lead to economic development and created immense wealth. However on its own this does not turn a nation into a world power. Whilst China has become the world's factory, this is all at the lower end of the technology ladder. The Atlantic monthly writer James Fallows spent a year in China, watching the nation's industrial machine up close. He compared China's current manufacturing capability to the U shaped smile on a happy face, he illustrated the development of a product, from its initial conception to its eventual sale. At the top left of the curve there is the initial idea and industrial design, the products details and how it will eventually look and work. Lower down the on the curve is the detailed plan by an engineer. At the bottom of the curve is the manufacturing, assembly and shipping. Then rising up on the right of the curve is the distribution, marketing, retail, sale, service contracts, parts and accessories. Fallows observed that in almost all the manufacturing industry in China, China takes care of the bottom of the curve and the US the top. He said: *"The simple way to put this – that the real money is in the brand name, plus retail."* The ends of the U is where the money is and the US dominates this area globally. China is fast going down the road Japan ended in. Throughout the 1980'S Japan was meant to overtake the US economy and replace it as the world's superpower, similar to China it became the worlds industrial factory, in the end the Asian financial crisis of 1997 proved the fallacy of what an export led policy actually leads to.

China's rapid economic development has been anything but equal. The Special Economic Zone's (SEZ) were all constructed on China's Eastern coast and everything that comes of the production line is placed on ships as cargo and exported to the world. The coastal region as a result is interlinked with the global economy; it has seen most of China's rapid development and enriched a new breed of elites, all at the expense of the rest of China. A large chunk of China today remains largely agrarian, has little infrastructure and lives in poverty. This has created China's massive internal cohesion problem.

For centuries, China has attempted to hold together a vast multi-cultural and multi-ethnic nation despite periods of political centralization and fragmentation. But cultural and linguistic differences have worsened due to uneven growth and a massive misdistribution of wealth. Physical mistreatment, imprisonment, lax labour laws and pitiful pay and the fact that the Chinese government is seen not to have addressed the economic needs of the vast bulk of the population is causing internal strife and calls for political succession. In 2005 China handled 87,000 cases of social unrest; this is public disturbances, demonstrations and civil strife. Domestically China is a very unstable society.

China domestically is ruled by Communism in all but name, this is why it still has a one party system, it has been unable to shrug off the legacy of its communist past, while embracing capitalism. At the same time China is nationalist led which has led to calls for separation by some regions. Until China decides what its national identity is, the nation will continue to be pulled in different directions and China will never be able to pose a threat to the world's superpower. The imposition of the ethnic Hans over the other ethnicities only contributes towards the problem. If the US felt China poses an immediate threat to its interests it could with much ease support one of the minority groups and cause internal problems for China.

Conclusions

China's rapid economic growth has for long worried the US, its economic strength could be turned into political ambitions and threaten the US. The US has for the most part worked to contain China in its region and on some issues engaged with it in order to control it. Currently China posses an economic challenge to the US, but as of yet has shown little political threat to the world's superpower. China is currently looking to strengthen itself in the region and this allows it to deal with its number one priority – societal cohesion.

Chinese policy makers and the army do have ambitions for China to be the world's superpower and this is why the US is designated a threat by most from the Chinese communist party, however Chinese tools to counteract the US are currently limited to its economic card as that is all the Chinese currently have until they are able to develop their military and political views about the world. China does not aim to be the only superpower, and does not mind co-existing with other powers. China has not indicated that it wants to establish an order in the world led by itself or its principles, which other superpowers throughout history have done.

Due to China's human capital its potential on the world staged cannot be ruled out. It has a sphere of influence and is able to buy off interests in countries across the world. It is able to resist and withstand pressures very well with its seat on the G20 and the UN. With all of this China is comfortable with being a power amongst many powers in the world.

US central intelligence estimates and quadrennial reviews constantly propose the US to increase military expenditure in the face of Chinese threats. China as a threat to the US is overblown when China is still on the early part of asserting itself on the world and has not shown any signs of wanting to replace the existing order.

Currently China only poses an economic challenge to the US, with the potential to pose a political alternative to US domination. For these reasons it is unlikely China will be replacing the US in the short to medium term as the world's superpower.

17 October 2016
Adnan Khan

Chapter 2

Chinese GeoPolitical Dynamics

Russia – China Relations - Rapprochement Or Rivalry

Russian & Chinese joint military manoeuvres

Question: On the 25th of August 2005, the common Chinese-Russian manoeuvres, in which different types of forces such as ships, marines, bombers, helicopters, fighting planes participated, came to an end… does this signify that a serious closeness is being born between China and Russia? And what effect does it have on the European Union and America?

Answer: Some military Russian and Chinese forces began common military manoeuvres in the period between 18-25 august 2005. They began in Vladivostic, far east of Russia, then moved to the Chinese territories in the peninsula of Shan Dong. Different forces participated in these manoeuvres, their number came to 10 thousand in each army. The manoeuvres included ground, air and marine work in the yellow sea in front of Shang Dong province, some of these works were: training on sea siege, evacuation operations and also fighting against "common threat". These manoeuvres were given the name of "peace mission 2005". These manoeuvres were so intense that they became so obvious as Russia has always had bad relations with China since the Soviet Union when Khruschev made an agreement with Kennedy in 1961. It was so unexpected that such negotiations will take place between Russia and China until the beginning of this year's spring when the Russian prime minister, Yuri Palovisky, visited Peking and at the end of his talks with his Chinese homologue, Lyang, he declared that Russia and China have agreed "on carrying out their first common military plan next autumn" according to what Al-Jazeera net published in 18.03.2005.

To realize the effect of these plans, we must go backwards a little bit to see that the American policy towards China meant imposing isolation on it and putting obstacles that would prohibit the expansion of China's international relations. America succeeded in 1989 on imposing embargo on the exportation of weapons from America and the EU to China following the oppression of Chinese tanks to the students' movement in Peking. America also created problems for China each time it developed an international commercial relation. America's international control continued especially in the beginning of the nineties when the Soviet Union collapsed and America became an international star and Europe walked with America (with harmony) except for a few simple troubles from Britain behind the scenes. American policy continued in isolating China on the international level and it blockade on her economically and military, this policy carried on successfully somehow with the support of Europe. However, some of the events of the 11th September 2001 and the American arrogance in (attacking the world) and its negligence of Europe's opinion concerning the attack on Iraq, then -and which is the most important- drowning in the dilemma of Afghanistan and Iraq, all that created a suitable atmosphere for Europe to (disturb) America and knock on the hot doors which affect her, some of these doors were:

1. It started founding justifications for not continuing the weapon embargo on China,
2. Russia began also to originate gatherings with China and some of the countries of central Asia to confront the American influence in the region, the result of that was the conference of Shanghai.
3. Then these great manoeuvres between China and Russia.

As for the attempts of the EU to raise the embargo on weapons, it started with the decision of the head of the presidents of the EU in December 2004 which included "to work on raising the embargo on the weapons on China by the end of June 2005." This issue was stirred strongly since March of this year, especially in June of this year, and during the conference of the European summit to an extent which disturbed America clearly. Shroeder and Chirac had adopted this idea -raising the embargo-, Shroeder declared in his speech in front of the German parliament in the middle of this year

"I am convinced that the embargo became one of the issues which could be cancelled -an extra matter- because China today is no more China of 1989." Before that and in March of this year during the last visit of Chirac to Japan, he declared in a press conference with the Japanese prime minister, saying "there's no fear of resuming the selling of European weapons for China as long as the matter is not concerned with delicate weapons or technology." After that, Chirac called the Chinese prime minister as was reported by the new Chinese news agency saying "it is a must to cancel the old embargo of selling European weapons because that will help in encouraging the relations between China and the EU." As was reported by Al-Jazeera on 02.04.2005.

It was obvious that these declarations were to encourage the international relations with China and were a strike for the American intentions in isolating China. America considered this issue as a challenge, as the minister of state for foreign affairs in Washington, Nicholas Berns, described raising the embargo by saying "it is a direct challenge for the interests of the U.S.A" and the minister of foreign affairs, Rice, considered it "a wrong indication" as was reported by the German financial times on the internet on 16.04.2005.

2. As for Russia originating gatherings with China in the face of America and its influence in central Asia was the gathering of Shanghai which includes Russia, China, Kazakhstan, Kyrgyzstan, Tajikistan and Uzbekistan. The summit of Shanghai announced last June what was considered a challenge for America in central Asia, and the announcement of the summit was "demanding Washington to renew the time of the evacuation of its bases in central Asia." After that, Bakayeiv, president of Kyrgyzstan, and after beginning his presidential missions, demanded to hasten the evacuation of the American bases in his country. Also Karimov, president of Uzbekistan, demanded America to evacuate its bases and fix a 6 months period for that. Although America tried to originate an antagonistic

gathering from its allied countries in the region, (such as Ukraine, Georgia, Poland and Lithuania) yet the gathering of "Shanghai" was more effective.

3. After that came the manoeuvres of the Chinese Russian forces which was a strike in the heart for the American path towards China. Although the military leaders in both countries tried to emphasize that these manoeuvres do not carry a threat for anyone, yet it's happening so intensely and specially that Washington wasn't invited to attend these manoeuvres as a supervisor according to what the traditions of peace relations among the disputing countries require. Add to that what accompanied these manoeuvres from a distant American supervision and what was issued by the Pentagon concerning it. Washington increased its supervision in the region of the pacific ocean near the site of the Chinese-Russian manoeuvres, at a time when the Pentagon resources declared its special concern about the missions of using the Russian strategic missiles and the experiments of shooting missiles which crossed the continents and using plane carriers in these manoeuvres.

Thats why what was declared by "Jean Kanrojen", professor of the international relations at the Chinese national university, by saying "the first aim of these manoeuvres is the United Nations because both sides want to improve its negotiating positions concerning security policy and economy." which is a saying that has a great deal of truth. From what mentioned, it is clear that these manoeuvres is a disturbance or more for America, and a strong strike for the policy of America towards China because these manoeuvres mean making China a partner in the international impact and not to keep it isolated from the international theatre. It also indicates the wavering situation of America because of its crises in Iraq and Afghanistan, or else Russia and China wouldn't have dared to challenge it in such a way to the extent that it wasn't invited as a supervisor.

Two points concerned with the question are left:

The first: About the attitude of the EU, it clearly encourages the disturbance of America especially by Chirac then Shroeder. Also Britain isn't absent from this struggle, it stands behind the scenes to inflame it whenever there is an opportunity to do so. For example, it was Britain which encouraged its allies in Australia to improve its relations with China and to raise the embargo on weapons, it also encouraged the well noticed Indian closeness to China under the rule of its agents from the Congress party. Aljazeera reported on 02.06.2005 "China, India and Russia emphasized in the meeting of their foreign ministers in Bladifustot at the far east of Russia that it wants to cooperate in order to guarantee stability in the region. This is besides what was obvious from the attitude of Europe concerning the manoeuvres where it considered it from the affairs of the sovereignty of the countries. All that shows that the European Union, France, Germany and Britain, encourages such deeds.

The second: what was stated in the question about the serious closeness between Russia and China? Declarations were published which insinuates that the closeness is serious, such as the declaration of the general chief of the Chinese military forces "these manoeuvres will consolidate the relations between Moscow and Peking and it also will lead to a kind of military unity between the 2 armies or the 2 countries in confronting any mutual danger." But what is nearer to reality that what happened is a harmony of interests, China wants to get out of its isolation that is to have international impact, and Russia wants to draw the attention for its being a power which has balance and to make America fear it in the international policy especially in Central Asia, that is why this closeness was a result of periodic circumstances and not strategic circumstances. As for the declaration of the chief general or other military officers, they are not political declarations, therefore such declarations about the unity of the army or the 2 countries shouldn't be taken seriously.

23 Rajab 1426 AH
28 August 2005 CE

India-Pakistan Relations in Light of US Policy and its affect on China

Question:

US President was one of the first to congratulate the victory of Janata Party and its leader Modi, where he has invited him to visit Washington; so it was announced on 05/06/2014 that Modi will make this visit in the month of September. The inauguration of India's new Prime Minister, Modi, took place on 26/05/2014 after the announcement of landslide victory of his party, Bharatiya Janata Party (BJP), with 282 seats of the total 545 seats in the parliament's seats, except two seats to be elected by the president, inflicting a heinous historic defeat to the Indian Congress party, which won 44 seats. It is for the first time that the Prime Minister of Pakistan to attend such a ceremony, following Modi's invitation to him to attend it and to meet with him. What are the implications of that? And how will the relations between the two countries pursue within the US policy and plans in relation to the two countries and the region and its impact on China and Afghanistan?

Answer:

1. American support for Modi had been remarkable during the elections. The campaign polishing Modi was not only run in India but extended to the wide range of Hindu sympathetic organizations residing outside the country, especially in America, which sought to promote "Modi" as a leader for all Indians and who is willing to work with minorities without exception. Among those organizations that stood by Modi's side; American India Foundation and US India Political Action Committee (USINPAC). These organizations did not fail to coordinate and cooperate with the arms following the BJP directly or indirectly, such as the Foreign Affairs Cell and

the Overseas Friends of BJP, not to mention thousands of Indians living in America and elsewhere.

Perhaps what confirms this overwhelming support for the party is what was published by the American Enterprise Institute in Washington that most of the funds raised abroad to finance the election campaign was drawn to BJP, and that more than ten thousand Indians holding American and European nationalities and support policies that are incentives for companies and market economy, flocked to India during the election campaign, to support Modi and urged voters to give him their votes. Of course, this momentum generated by the dense support of the party friends and the supporters of its policies and the supporters of Modi and his allies, had a big role in upholding him and the marginalization of the rest of the election campaigns of other parties.

In any case, it is clear that the pressing interest of America in the Far East was behind the winning of the fanatical Hindu Modi. Thus, it came in an article published by the BBC Arabic on 19th May 2014 under the title "Viewpoints: How will Modi affect US-India relations?" As quoted in the article under the title "Doing business with Mr. Modi" by Lisa Curtis, Heritage Foundation: "New Delhi and Washington share strategic objectives, whether it involves fighting terrorism, maintaining open seaways, or hedging against China's rise. Specifically the BJP interest in adopting a more assertive hedging policy regarding China will give US officials a chance to engage closely with them". Also, US President Barack Obama urged Modi to visit the United States when he telephoned him on Friday to congratulate him on his victory; according to a statement issued by the White House. Obama said he looks forward to working closely with Modi to "fulfill the extraordinary promise of the US-India strategic partnership". According to the report published by the BBC in Arabic, on 16th May 2014, Obama said that "the President invited Modi to visit Washington at a mutually agreeable time to further strengthen the bilateral relations between the two countries."

2. Thus we have seen a US eagerness for the victory of the Modi-led Janata Party immediately after the elections and before the announcement of the final and official results. It was mentioned in the *Middle East* Newspaper on 12/05/2014: "Obama praised the Indian elections which just ended on 12/05/2014 with the release of preliminary results that shows the winning of the BJP, advancing the final results on 16/05/2014", saying, "We look forward to the formation of a new Indian government to work closely with India's next administration to make the coming years equally transformative..." This indicates the willingness of America for the Bharatiya Janata Party, led by Modi to win in order to cooperate with it, like when the party cooperated with it when headed by Atal Bihari Vajpayee when he was in power during the period between 1998 and 2004.

And now as well, when the victory of this party was officially announced on 16/05/2014, Obama congratulated its leader Modi in a telephone call, and invited him to visit Washington and meet him. The US President indicated in his telephone conversation with Modi that he was "looking forward to working closely with Modi to push the extraordinary and the promising US-India strategic partnership." And "agreed to continue to expand and deepen cooperation on a large scale." (The Indian NDTV, 17/05/2014). On 05/06/2014, two Indian newspapers namely, *Times of India* and *Hindustan Times* published news that Modi's visit to Washington will be in September to meet US President. All this indicates that America is confident of the progress of India under the leadership of this party, headed by its leader Modi, under the name of exceptional strategic partnership. News agents reported at an earlier date this year, the news of meetings of US Ambassador to India with the leader of the Janata Party, Modi, before the elections, indicating the drawing of shared plans that Modi to follow after his election in accordance with the US policy.

America cheered for the victory of Modi and the return of BJP to power, after ten years of rule by the Congress party, where the India-America relations in its era were not so good, since it did not respond much with America especially on the subject of confronting China. That's why Obama rushed the election results in India and announced his delight for the return of the American agents to power. His delight has made him forget the American decision to ban Modi from entering the United States because of the massacres of Muslims in Gujarat when Modi was its Chief Minister. And in this a lesson for those deceived by what America claims of human rights. As America strikes all human rights if this is in their own interest. Thus, America's decision to ban Modi has become a warm welcome for his victory and a ceremonial case for Modi's upcoming visit to the United States...

Accordingly, the United States at the height of its ecstasy for the return of the Janata Party to rule, since those loyal to America became the rulers in India and Pakistan. So it is expected for America to ask its agents in Pakistan, led by Prime Minister Nawaz Sharif to provide more concessions to India to strengthen its position i.e. the position of India in the face of China. In other words, US want to stop the state of conflict between Pakistan and India, but at the expense of Pakistan... The main issue that weighs heavily on the bilateral relations is the disputed Kashmir region, followed by the presence of armed Islamic groups active in India, which New Delhi accuses Pakistan of supporting them. It is expected that America would press on its agent Nawaz Sharif to make significant and dangerous concessions for the benefit of India in Kashmir to appease the Hindu extremist, Narendra Modi, and his party. And that America will press on Nawaz Sharif to pursue the militants in Kashmir to eradicate the so-called terrorism, so that it is able to make India focus on confronting the rising China.

The like of this has occurred when the BJP was in power between the years 1998 and 2004, where Pakistan made concessions in Kashmir in favor of India to strengthen American agents there and enhance its influence. Thus, Nawaz Sharif ordered the Pakistani army to withdraw from the Heights of Kargil after being liberated by the army and the Mujahideen in their heroic battles. This was after Nawaz Sharif visited US and met its president at that time, Bill Clinton on 04/07/1999. So, America pressured him to withdraw from it, and so he succumbed and ordered the withdrawal... Nawaz now continues in concessions, and the harbingers of that is that Nawaz Sharif took part in the inauguration ceremony of India's new prime minister, Modi, on 26/5/2014 and his meeting with him for an hour and a half during which Modi told him that: "Pakistan must prevent militants from using its soil to attack India and punish the perpetrators of the attack on Mumbai in 2008". (Reuters, 27/05/2014) But Nawaz Sharif showed weakness and subservience; he did not correspond by a response at the level equal to that, but he merely told reporters, "He held a warm and cordial bilateral meeting with Modi". He says these words, while still the events of Indian state of Gujarat are present in the minds of Muslims. In 2002, when Narendra Modi became a chief minister of Gujarat, the Hindus did atrocities against Muslims led to the deaths of more than 2,000 Muslims and the displacement of about 100 thousands of them and they continue to suffer the repercussions of this displacement and did not return to their homes. The territorial Government did not help them or the Central Government of India, and also did not raise the issue of India's support for separatists in Balochistan province of Pakistan. Thus, instead of Nawaz Sharif addressing the India's new Prime Minister, Modi, and at least throwing all this at his face, rather he was week in front of him in accordance to the requirements of the American policy of making Pakistan appease India!

3. On the other hand, it appears that America is giving a role for India in Afghanistan and works to strengthen relations between the two countries so as not to remain in need of Pakistan to promote stability. Hence, the first

president that Modi met at his inauguration was Karzai of Afghanistan. Thus, America trusts India when the Government is loyal to it; as is the case now, more than its trust in Pakistan. Although the government in Pakistan is loyal to it, but is afraid that any change may happen in this Muslim country at any moment, so it is unsafe for it in the long run. Its people are in the move for change, and there is a real and serious tendency towards liberation and freedom from the West in general and in particular, America, which has authority over the ruling regime and brings agent rulers, in addition to its holding of the army leadership. And so America has created pillars for itself in the political and military leadership in Pakistan. And America fears that the Ummah could destroy all what it had built of pillars, and its biggest fear is that the Ummah to establish the rule of Islam and declare Khilafah, and this is what worries America. Therefore, America is not content with relying on the regime in Pakistan to sort things in Afghanistan, after achieving the "withdrawal" of American soldiers from it, but wants to make India to have an active role in Afghanistan in sorting of those situations; through promoting security cooperation between India and Afghanistan and its dependence more on India in terms of security after the withdrawal of US and Western forces from there. The Christian Science Monitor published on 01/06/2014 a report on India-Afghanistan relations saying that, "When Afghanistan President Hamid Karzai attended the inauguration ceremony of India's new prime minister, Narendra Modi, last week he brought an impressive wish list including battle tanks, field guns, trucks and military helicopters". The newspaper added, "Karzai's requests coincides with a growing debate within Indian government and military circles whether New Delhi would ramp up its military aid to Kabul or not..." The paper adds, "India shares traditionally warm ties with Afghanistan. After shunning Afghanistan during the Taliban regime, India became a friend and a strategic partner". Therefore, India in the era of the American loyal, Modi, will play an active role in terms of security in Afghanistan in favor of the American loyal regime there.

4. With regard to China, its influence has increased over the past two decades, where it worked to strengthen itself in the region. The United States is working to curb China through countries that surround it, such as Japan, South Korea, Vietnam and India. That is why the United States has various alliances and partnerships in order to contain China and occupy it with those states on its borders. America saw India in the subcontinent as a suitable state to confront China, because of its previous enmity with China about various border disputes.

Thus, America wants India to be used effectively to increase pressure on China in order to curb it and prevent it from dominating the surrounding areas and keep it confined to its territory and occupied with India and the protection of its borders. Therefore America announced its plan two years ago that relates to the Asia-Pacific region. Part of this policy was the mobilization of about 60% of its naval force to counter China in the region and the establishment of alliances with countries in the region to mobilize them beside it and direct them to act against China. Among these countries was India, so it worked on directing it towards the east area in the Pacific; specifically in the area of the South China Sea and tempted it by the presence of energy sources of oil and gas. However, the Government of India, led by the Congress Party did not respond much with America in this trend. This, despite the fact that America put all its weight in order to attract Congress Party-led India, where it sent its Vice President Joseph Biden, as well as Secretary of State John Kerry in the middle of last year for this purpose. It also prompted Australia to establish a partnership with India, and pressed Pakistan to make concessions to India including the withdrawal of its troops from the border area with India so that India can move its troops and concerns around the border with China. George W. Bush had visited India in March 2006 at the time of the Congress party, and signed many agreements supportive of India, including in the field of development of nuclear energy for peaceful purposes, as well as the Obama visit to India in November 2010; all to influence the ruling Congress Party in India and to tempt it towards US policy. However, America has not been able to influence it to make it march within the American policy in the region or to be an effective partner besides it in the implementation of its policy. This is due to the loyalty of India's Congress party to the English, and its criticism of US policy. The statement of the party in the 2005 elections clearly indicates this, in which it came: "It is sad that a great country like India has declined to the level of having a relationship of adherence to the United States of America, where the government of the United States of America considers the adherence of India a given. This has led to the BJP government being prepared to adapt to the priorities and policies of the United States of America without due consideration to India's vital foreign policy and national security interests."

Thus, America did not succeed in convincing the Congress Party in the implementation of America's policy towards China. In addition to that, the United States has failed to make the Indian military leadership focus on developing its army away from Pakistan, and its concentration towards China. Thus the Indian army is focused on internal stability, Kashmir and its borders with Pakistan. With seven of the India's nine armies in addition to three brigades are deployed along the border with Pakistan. Besides, 80% of the front main bases are directed against Pakistan.

Having the BJP win the election in May 2014 - the party that has always been loyal to the United States since the time of Vajpayee in the nineties- it had given another chance for America to put India in confrontation with China. As the greatest obstacle to make India confront China is the presence of the Congress party in power. This obstacle has now disappeared, so it has become easier for America to convince the BJP, which is loyal to it, to concentrate the Indian army on the borders of China instead of the border with Pakistan. Particularly that the United States ensure the Janata Party that Pakistani leadership will focus the Pakistani Army towards northern areas and reduce its numbers and ordnance on the Indian border, due to the subordination of the military and political leadership in Pakistan to the US requirements...! Also it is worth noting that, the Pakistani army is organized primarily into 13 corps, nine of them are deployed near the Indian border. Since Musharraf and Kayani, the military operations in the Northern regions and the Swat area led to the transfer of some of these corps away from the Indian border.

In January 2013, General Kayani announced the strategic principle of the country. Accordingly, the military situation has been modified, and has determined that the internal threats are the greatest threat to the security of the country and not India. Consequently, Pakistan transferred the center of its attention from the borders of India to the northern areas of Pakistan bordering Afghanistan. However, this step from Pakistan was not met by a similar step from India, rather it continued to see Pakistan as a major threat to it, and was reluctant to move its troops completely away from the border with Pakistan.

On the whole, now that the regimes in India and Pakistan have come to implement US policy, America will continue to occupy Pakistan with the issue of Afghanistan and the Northern areas, and then there will be no justification for the major presence of the Indian military on the border with Pakistan, and will allow India to focus on confronting China. For this reason, the United States will provide military equipment to India through security deals, and with the presence of BJP now in power, a party that is for a long time wanted to play the role of policeman of the subcontinent, it will continue proceeding along this path. It is expected that America to present to India economic transactions such as investment in Indian companies, and the transfer of technology to help the economy of India. It is likely that the Bharatiya Janata Party (BJP) will highlight its military expansion by seeking energy in the South China Seas.

America is interested in promoting strategic cooperation to curb China and neutralize its activity by putting it under control. The emergence of India as a rival to China and in particular that the BJP had won the election with majority votes, which enables it to be a single party in power, this facilitates the way for America to move India towards China, particularly in the following areas:

a. Stirring the issue of the independence of Tibet, and the dispute taking place between China and India on the border of Ladakh region.

b. Trade routes; that is the security aspect of the trade routes passing through the China Sea, which constitute 50% of the international shipping. All these create problems that will occupy China in solving them; hence they confine it in the surrounding areas in accordance with the planned US policy towards China. It seems that America has succeeded in moving Modi toward China. Thus, Modi has appointed former commander of the Army P. K. Singh, a federal minister for the Northeastern area to reform the national security there, which Modi says that it became weak under the previous government, as well as to deal with China. Singh told reporters after assuming charge in his new post last Thursday, "The development of the North East will be my extreme priority." It is expected that Singh may bring back attention to India's plan to create a force of 80 thousand troops along the border with China in the North-East.

Thus, the United States is proceeding with its plan to move India towards China after securing the borders of India on the Pakistani side, where it orders the Pakistani leadership to direct the Pakistani army to the border with Afghanistan and the Northern regions to enter into a fight with its Muslim brothers. Rather than to draw the attention of the military to lift the captivity of Kashmir and liberate it as obliged by Allah and made it a duty on Muslims not to allow the enemies of Allah to have authority over any of the Muslim countries.

"And never will Allah give the disbelievers over the believers a way [to overcome them]."
[An-Nisa: 41].

America in its crimes, plots and violation of the States, have surpassed notorious colonists ... It is for the sake of its own colonial interests, it has no qualms about any crime and conspiracy. It conspires against China openly, and conspires against India in a covert way, so it perceives that standing in the face of China by land and sea is in the interest of India and tempts it with aid and strategic agreements, but all that would harm India in the end since China is stronger financially and ideologically.... However, China and India have nothing in common to gather them, thus for them to fight is not odd. But what is strange is that both regimes in Pakistan and Afghanistan are implementing US policy which requires the Muslims in Pakistan and Afghanistan to fight each other... and the most surprising that these two oppressor regimes are still authoritative on people's necks! The duty of this Ummah that Allah glorified them with Islam is to adhere and rule by Islam, and to remove these regimes, and re-establish the Islamic state, the rightly guided Khilafah. So it tramples America and its plots, and return Afghanistan and Pakistan, and all Muslim countries servants of Allah as one brotherhood,

*"And that day the believers will rejoice * In the victory of Allah. He gives victory to whom He wills, and He is the Exalted in Might, the Merciful."*   [Ar-Rum: 4-5]

13th Sha'ban 1435 AH
11 June 2014 CE

North Korea & China – Comrades in Arms?

Question: What could be understood from what was announced that North Korea performed a nuclear experiment? Did it really perform this experiment or is it a news media stimulation, which was produced well for a political aim?

Answer: It is known that Korea is a nuclear country, meaning that it has the scientific as well as the financial ability. The Soviet Union used to help it before the Kennedy -Khrushchev agreement in 1961, after that, when the relation of the Soviet Union deteriorated with China- China continued its support. At the beginning the aim of North Korea -from the strong arming and nuclear activity- was to re unite Korea. In return, America used to make military and economic agreements… with South Korea in order to prevent that.

After the relations between America and China, the Chinese support for Korea -in order to reach the aim of re-uniting Korea- became less, then the (momentum) of arming Korea became a burden on its economy, the aim was not to take South Korea, but to protect its own entity, especially that its economic resources became nearly scarce, it wanted to decrease the arming and be more interested in its economy, but it also wanted to guarantee the safety of its entity, knowing that danger is coming from America, so it started provocations to draw the attention and to sign an agreement with America (not to assault) and organize an economic status (aids) with South Korea and Japan, knowing that this will be accomplished if it signed an agreement with America, because it is the stimulus for the neighboring countries.

America refused the mutual negotiations, and agreed on the six fold negotiations, so that the neighboring countries will share in the issue, and so that enmity will not be limited between America and North Korea, but to have hostile sides from the neighbors (supposed enemies). Thus Korea was not able to realize what it wanted.

Provoking the nuclear experiment (the last experiment) is a political work, to force America to negotiate with North Korea and to originate an agreement of security and peace and guarantee its entity, upon which America will sign, so that Korea will attend to its economic situation.

This means that the original aim from the intensive arming of North Korea -which was to unite both Koreas- had deteriorated from the side of the Soviet Union since 1961, and from the side of China since the mid-nineties, when warmth stirred to a certain extent in the relations between America and China.

Hence, North Korea wants to guarantee the survival of its entity, in order to attend to improving the standard of its economy, this requires making a mutual agreement with America concerning that. America wants the agreements to be discussed by the countries of the region, so that its commitment will be not binding (be loose).…. Therefore the nuclear actions (and the provocations in the gulf of Korea) were for drawing the attention, to warm the atmosphere and make America agree on signing a mutual agreement with it.

As for inquiring about the experiment, it really took place, but it was not that big to cause dangerous radiation, especially that the regions in which the experiments are allowed are close to China. And Korea has no one left to lean on except China.

And because China is no more in a state of hostility with America as before, there are even economic interests through some American companies… therefore it is expected that china will not aggravate the situation, and that it will resume the six fold negotiations in order to achieve a compromise according to the capitalist method, as for signing a direct mutual agreement between America and Korea in other than the atmosphere of the six fold negotiations, this will not exist at least in the range of vision.

One probability remains, which is that the current economy of North Korea is very weak, it gets funds from China and (some) from south Korea, it wants to guarantee its entity to lessen the expenditure on its arming and stress on its economy instead…. But if things remain as they are, and it does not get an agreement with America to guarantee its security and stop aggression…. Meaning if it is jammed in the corner…. Then there is a possibility to make a bigger provoking action -a more dangerous one- to reach to an agreement with America. But this probability is made weak by the attitude of China -which has effect on Korea- which puts pressure on North Korea, being the main source of economic support, with what its gives from aids to Korea.

Therefore things will be directed towards the six fold committee and compromises will be done with America, in which there is face saving for the sides which have association.

01 Shawal 1427 AH
23 October 2006 CE

North Korea's Nuclear Weapons Development and Chinese Diplomacy

Question:

It is apparent from this that while the statements of a heated war are escalating, so are the statements of dialogue. Therefore where are matters heading? What then are the actual positions of Russia and China? May Allah reward you.

Answer:

In order to understand this issue, we have to review it from its beginning, not on the basis of the latest statements alone, this issue has passed many stages which we will outline first, and then outline the recent developments and the positions of the States:

1. This crisis did not erupt as a result of yesterday's events, but is a frequent one, and it escalates at every nuclear experiment carried out by North Korea. It escalated at the first experiment in the year 2006, as well as at the second one in the year 2009 which was greater than the first. At that time, dated 25/5/2009, North Korea announced that it is not bound to the truce signed between them and America in the year 1953. Now that a third nuclear test has been successfully performed on 12/02/2013, it also announced on 30/03/2013 that it will not comply with the truce, and declared that it is in a state of war. North Korea then began to focus its missiles off the east coast directing them towards Japan and the U.S. base on the island of Guam, which is controlled by America in the Pacific Ocean since 1898 after it defeated Spain which occupied Guam since 1521; in the year 1950, America declared its annexation to its territory, and deemed the population of more than 180 thousand people as part of its population, which is used for military bases for the Army and Navy and includes approximately 6000 of its

soldiers. Thus Guam is considered significant because it serves as a line of defense for its territory from the Pacific Ocean side.

2. What is new this time is that America was able to provoke North Korea with conducting large maneuvers near North Korea. These maneuvers began on 19/2/2013 and will continue until the end of this month 30/4/2013; these maneuvers are large and unprecedented, coinciding with the sanctions set by America in the Security Council, which were approved by Russia and China on 7/3/2013, after the West and America in particular stirred efficiently North Korea's third experiment on 12/2/2013. These maneuvers created an intense provocation to North Korea, as they were of an unusual nature, which in these maneuvers America introduced advanced types of forces from B-52 aircrafts as well as B-2 that are capable of carrying nuclear bombs, including stealth aircraft and warships carrying a missile system as a way of exhibiting their strength to terrorize North Korea and other countries.

3. The sanctions and maneuvers are a continuation of the techniques of evasion and deception, pressure and threat carried out by America in the region. As for the techniques of evasion and deception carried out by America towards North Korea, for example, North Korea has agreed last year in 02/29/2012 to suspend its nuclear program and allowed the return of inspectors, therefore America sent 240 thousand tons of aid to the North during the first nuclear experiment performed after the death of its leader Kim Jong Il and his son Kim Jong-un came to rule. In the process of evasion and deception to stop the aid, America rose and accused the leaders of the North that they kept these aids to themselves and denied the people of it, thereby as a form of humiliation to North Korea portraying them as beggars and that the officials steal these aids. As for the methods of challenge, pressure and threat used by the United States, it announced last year a new strategy in the Asia / Pacific region regarding strengthening its power in this region by transferring 60% of its Navy forces to cope with potential risks until 2020.

All of these methods used by America were to provoke North Korea to behave in a heated manner while in contrast; they are used by America as a justification to expand their bases near China and Russia in the region under the pretext of resisting danger of North Korea. What concerns for America in the first degree is China, and in the subsequent degree, Russia ... and not North Korea, and the expansion of the U.S. presence near China which will face a Chinese reaction, and a lighter Russian reaction. If there were an excuse for America, especially if it perfected its exploitation, it would then be able to expand militarily and even set up a missile shield without causing any hostile fuss.

4. This is what has happened, these provocations affected North Korea and thus propelling it to a heated escalation against America and its neighbors South Korea and Japan. On 9/3/2013, North Korea waved once again the outbreak of war in the region when its official agency published a press release saying: "The Korean Peninsula is heading towards a heated-nuclear war." This agency also published on 3/4/2013 a communique to the North Korean forces that mentioned: "The American threats will be destroyed with smaller, lighter and more versatile nuclear weapons," and that the army "had received an approval to strike America with the possibility of using nuclear weapons that are sophisticated and diverse." It also announced the cancellation of the truce between them and America since the year 1953.

Thereafter, North Korea worked on escalating the situation to the maximum, so it demanded from Russia, Britain and other countries to evacuate their embassies from the country; and called on foreigners to leave South Korea if events escalated; and placed mid-range missiles on the platforms launch and concealed them on the east coast in a move that suggests that they threaten Japan and U.S. bases in the Pacific. It responds to the maneuvers and sanctions imposed on it by the United Nations. It also closed the industrial zone in Kaesong Industrial Complex where companies station South North workers and generated an income that exceeded half a billion dollars last year, an area set up by South Korea motivated by North

America as a way to contain the North. The establishment of the inter-Korean industrial zone begun in late 2004, in accordance with a plan that initially started in 1998, which includes 123 South Korean companies, and employs nearly 54 thousand workers from North Korea. As a reaction to this tension with the United States and South Korea, North Korea announced on 02/04/2013 the rehabilitation and operation of all installations in the Yongbyon nuclear compound that was stopped in 2007, including a site for uranium enrichment and reactors of power level 5 MW, by doing this, North Korea aims to becoming accepted by America and the world as a country that has become a nuclear state, and has ballistic missiles able to defend itself and to threaten others.

5. America then took to exploiting these heated tensions resulting from the fiery statements of North Korea, so it took advantage of it to achieve its objective, which is to accelerate the deployment of the missile shield without causing any confrontation with Russia or China, alluring North Korea to find a justification for America to expand its presence in the region, which makes it seem as though it is doing so in defense of America and its allies, as Kerry said during a visit to South Korea on 12/04/2013.

After the threats of North Korea that it will strike the American bases with medium-range missiles owned by them, America announced as reported by The New York Times on 04/04/2013 that it "will establish a missile shield on this island to counter medium-range missiles, as well as the deployment of anti-ballistic missiles warships in the waters of the Pacific Ocean; it was scheduled to deploy their missile shield in 2015," the newspaper added: "The decision to accelerate the deployment of a missile defense system came under a series of steps taken by Washington to deter North Korea from carrying out any military action or new missile tests, the decision was taken after only a few hours of the North Korean provocations." The newspaper also added that "spreading the missile shield system in Guam will unleash the warships to become closer to sites near the North Korean seashore." This means that America will station near China, which points to America having benefited from its provocations with North Korea by hastening the spread of the missile shield in the region, and that it set a trap for North Korea so that it could achieve these objectives. As Japan announced its installment of Patriot missiles in the heart of the Capital to face North Korea's missiles and it will allow the installment of the missile system in Okynawa Island which has important American bases. With the fact that Japan had been calling for the expulsion of the Americans from there, and now Americans strengthen their presence with their bombardment of North Korea's threats without anyone's objections.

The Philippines announced its readiness to install this missiles system and strengthen the American presence on its land, although the people in the Philippines demanded an end to the American presence in the country.

6. As America was successful in exploiting the escalation of North Korea as a justification to expand the U.S. military presence and the deployment of the missile shield, America returned to its promised Democratic party policy, which is to contain North Korea through using dialogue the American way, i.e. not making the situation as an American-North Korean situation, but one that involves other countries in the region, in particular China, to become responsible for the actions of North Korea ... And this is what they have been doing, through the six-party talks, so the issue appears as if North Korea is facing the other five countries, and not America ...

It is worth mentioning that the Democrats' policy since Bill Clinton that the United States towards North Korea is to resort to negotiations with them, under their policy of containment, which was successful in 1994 when the first agreement was signed with North Korea, but America avoided, in the era of Republicans, particularly in the first period of Bush JR, making North Korea one of the states of the axis of evil. North Korea took a similar approach to what it did before conducting a nuclear test and declaring a non-compliance with the truce at the beginning of the first Obama administration in 2009, however, this administration did not respond to the North Korea provocations, but called for the resumption of negotiations and allowed South Korea to continue to work on the rapprochement with the North, for this reason, the Democratic administrations tend to negotiate with North Korea and implementation of the containment policy. The situation differs now, where America wanted to employ this latest event to achieve important strategic goals before entering into negotiations and pursuing the containment process, though this will begin after achieving its objectives that it had planned and still plans for since the announcement of installing the missile shield near the Korean peninsula.

Thus, the statements took a different turn but with conditions ... It is the American game that leads only to diluting the issue and making it spin in circles under the name of the six-party negotiations to ensure respect for North Korea's international commitments. [AFP 04/09/2013] The second in command official at the Pentagon, Ash Carter, said: "The United States is in close contact with China, Russia, South Korea and Japan," and he said that "he believes that China can play a greater role in influencing North Korea to stop its provocations," stressing "that China's influence on North Korea is greater than any other country." U.S. Secretary of State John Kerry mentioned in South Korea before heading to China: "The United States will never accept North Korea as a nuclear power." Stating, "It is up to Beijing to take a tougher stance with North Korea to push it towards abandoning its nuclear program." [Reuters: 12/04/2013] Thus, America wants to make the North Korea issue a regional issue especially with China, and not solely an American issue.

7. As for the position of China, it has changed this time from before; it did not support North Korea in its stride. The new Chinese president Ji Jin Ping said: "No country has the right to push Asia into chaos." And he added: "It is not allowed for anyone to push the region, or even the world, into chaos because of their selfishness." Also adding: "We should act in consultation to overcome major difficulties in order to ensure stability in Asia, which is facing new challenges, as long as there are sensitive issues and traditional and non-traditional security threats." [Middle East: 04/07/2013] China's

Foreign Minister Wan Bi called for "the need to resolve the crisis through dialogue." (same source) The Chinese Foreign Ministry spokesman Hong Lei has announced that "the best solution for the North Korean nuclear issue is for all parties to show responsibility." [Reuters: 8/4/2013] China has supported the Security Council resolution to toughen sanctions on North Korea after the latter conducted its third nuclear test. This does not mean that China has abandoned its friend North Korea, but it appears that China believes that the actions of North Korea may harm it and was disturbed by it, because it enhances the U.S. presence in the region and gives America excuses to establish a missile shield in the region as a whole and be directed against it and its missiles, eventually failing its plans of controlling its region.

China announced its regrets for the Pyongyang Declaration to restart the nuclear reactor. The International Atomic Energy Agency said that this declaration is another development, creating great regret and constitutes a flagrant violation of Security Council resolutions. This reactor is the only source for the production of plutonium for North Korea's nuclear program. It is likely that the North has plutonium stocks enough to make 4 or 8 nuclear bombs.

8. As for Russia's position, it takes the path as America, disapproving of North Korea's actions. Russian Foreign Ministry spokesman Alexander Ukashevic declared: "We stand in solidarity with them with respect to rejecting the approach of behavioral provocation and belligerent to Pyongyang at the moment." But he added at the same time that "we should not give up on making political and diplomatic efforts, because any country can bring the risk of severe turmoil in Northeast Asia." [Reuters: 09/04/2013] Russia has agreed to tightening sanctions on North Korea in the Security Council after the third experiment two months ago. Russia did not take serious measures towards the U.S. anti-North Korea position, and America's provocation against it by conducting maneuvers with South Korea while engaging its advanced weapons in these maneuvers, Russia therefore did not heed to it neither did they renounce it, knowing that this

poses danger for the region and aims to strengthen the U.S. presence in it to terrorize everyone and impose an American dominance on the world. It is directed against Russia itself in a way to disallow it to have any presence in this region. This behavior indicates the poor international political performance of Russia and it minimizes it to a level not worthy of a great state which has its own international interests and competes with the leading state or works on relegating it off this position.

9. So that, we can say that America was successful in provoking North Korea through the massive maneuvers conducted near North Korea and through sanctions, which led North Korea to escalating the nuclear threats and war atmosphere, which allowed America to find an excuse to expand its military presence in the region and the deployment of the missile shield.

However, the arrogance of America, that is arrogant with its strength makes its goals easily exposed, which allows China to realize the ploys of America's political and expansionist objectives in the region, and all this will make the installment of the missile shield enter into the spiral of the Chinese opposition from anew.

12 Jumada Al-Thani 1434 AH

22 April 2013 CE

India, Pakistan, China: Defense and nuclear tangle in South Asia

Pak-China-India relations

On his visit to Pakistan, the Chinese President Hu Jintao emphasised the importance of Sino-Pak relations and expressed his desire to expand bilateral ties between the two countries. "Let us build on past achievement and strengthen traditional friendship, advanced with the time, expand and enrich China-Pakistan strategic partnership so that our friendship will pass on from generation to generation," he said. The Pakistani government reciprocated by praising China's relationship with Pakistan. Colourful metaphors like "time-tested friendship" and "all weather friendship" were employed to convey this message to the Pakistani public. Supporters of the government pointed to the 18 agreements signed between the two countries as proof of China's longstanding commitment to Pakistan. These agreements included the much publicised Free Trade Agreement (FTA), the establishment of a free zone in Lahore for Chinese businesses, and a five year plan to boost bilateral trade between the two countries to $15 billion by 2011.

But beyond the media grabbing headlines and the over-inflated speeches by politicians—Pakistan's relationship with China has reached a crescendo and is unlikely to progress any further. In contrast, China's relationship with India has vastly improved and the two adversaries are exploring numerous partnerships to augment their newfound relationship. Prior to visiting Pakistan, Hu spent a few days in India and signed 13 agreements. These included protection of bilateral investment, trade of iron ore and the export of rice, agriculture cooperation, educational assistance, and the conservation of cultural heritage. Nevertheless the most obvious improvement in relations has been in bilateral trade. From a meagre US$117 million in the late eighties, the two-way trade for this year stands at $20 billion and is projected to reach $50 billion for 2010.

On the energy front the two nations instead of competing with each other are cooperating to meet the energy demands of their burgeoning economies. Indian and Chinese companies can be found collaborating on oil and gas projects in Iran, Syria, Sudan, Kazakhstan, South America and elsewhere in the world. While some of these joint ventures maybe small the trend supports the notion that China prefers to engage India over the acquisition and protection of energy resources. Commenting on the need of both countries to play an active role in shaping the international energy order, Prime Minister Manmohan Singh and President Hu said in a joint statement: "There is the need for an international energy order, and for global energy systems to take into account the needs of both countries based on a stable, predictable, secure and clean energy future. In this context, the international civilian nuclear cooperation should be advanced through innovative and forward-looking approaches while safeguarding the effectiveness of international non-proliferation principles."

On the nuclear front China has offered assistance to bolster India's nuclear energy for civilian purposes. The nuclear cooperation on offer is on more or less equivalent to what China has in place with Pakistan. Furthermore, Hu's refusal to commit to the building of extra nuclear reactors on his trip to Pakistan underscores China's intention of alluring India into a long-term nuclear partnership. On this note an interesting statement was issued by US State Department spokesman Sean McCormack in response to an Indian reporter who questioned whether China's nuclear help to Pakistan extended to civilian nuclear reactors. McCormack said there was no new nuclear agreement between Pakistan and China "other than what was already grandfathered in by the Nuclear Suppliers Group."

Drawing confidence from the emerging nuclear cooperation between the two countries, the Indians believe that China will not scupper India's bid to join the Nuclear Suppliers Group (NSG). Speaking on the matter External Affairs Minister Pranab Mukherjee said, "I am confident." Little wonder then that Manmohan Singh gave an upbeat assessment of Sino-Indian relations. He said," At the fulcrum of our efforts is our collective political will to enrich and reinforce our strategic and cooperative partnership for peace and prosperity, and to resolve our outstanding issues in a focused, sincere and problem-solving manner."

China and India have also made strides on defence matters. This includes port calls, joint search-and-rescue exercises and defence exchanges. Last year this relationship was upgraded when Beijing and New Delhi signed a memorandum of understanding on defence cooperation. While the military ties between the two countries are still in their infancy and do not quite match the military relationship found between China and Pakistan—it is more than evident that China is taking a different view of its one time adversary. Leaving boundary disputes aside, both countries are enjoying the benefits a multi-faceted bilateral relationship.

There are several reasons as to why Indian-Sino relations are expanding and maturing in comparison to Sino-Pak relations, which bear all the hallmarks of an association that is slowly becoming nominal.

Pakistan and September 11

In the aftermath of September 11, Pakistan adopted a more aggressive policy towards China. This policy disguised as the fight against terrorism enabled America to dislodge Taliban from power, appoint a puppet regime in Kabul and set up several military bases in Afghanistan. Moreover, Pakistan opened up it airspace to American fighter planes and under the pretext of search and rescue missions allowed the presence of a number of American air bases on Pakistani soil. Some of these air bases hosted several hundred American military personnel.

For the first time in many years, China perceived Pakistan to play an active role in cementing American hegemony adjacent to Chinese western borders—China now felt ensnared by America's military might stretching from the Asian Pacific rim to Afghanistan. Pakistan attempted to dispel these concerns by inviting China to invest in Gwadar the deep water port project in 2002. Pakistan promised China that Gwadar would facilitate the transport Chinese goods to Central Asia and give China access to the Arabian Sea and Middle Eastern markets. However, beyond the development of the port, China has shown little enthusiasm to utilise Gwadar as a gateway to these markets. The lack of interest is due to America's military presence in the region coupled with insurgencies in Balochistan and the tribal areas. China is also well aware of America's long-term plan to separate the Balochistan province from Pakistan and fuse it with Iran's Balochistan region creating Balochi state. Aspects of this plan have been mentioned in various US intelligence papers such as CIA paper on Global Trends in 2015.

China's has reacted to these developments by strengthening Shanghai Cooperation Organisation (SCO) and together with Russia is keeping the door firmly shut to any American intrusion into Central Asia from Afghanistan.

Normalisation between India and Pakistan

During the cold war China understood India's closeness to the Soviet Union as a threat to its security. To mitigate this danger, China extended its support to Pakistan— a defacto balance of power equation was pursued by China in

South Asia. However with the ascendancy of the pro-American BJP to power in India in the late nineties, and the ensuing normalistion process between India and Pakistan, China had to readjust its policy. China was now facing a combined threat from two pro-American countries. September 11 gave a fresh impetus to the normalisation process and magnified the threat posed by Pakistan and India to Chinese security. Beijing's hitherto policy of balance of power slowly gave way to a policy of 'engage and contain' India and Pakistan—both countries under American auspices were being groomed to act as a counterweight against China.

This meant that China had to carefully recalibrate its relationship with Pakistan, so as not to undermine its traditional sensitivities with Islamabad and yet, at the same time make overtures to India to gain her trust. India being much bigger than Pakistan required China to invest more time, effort and money not only to engage India, but also to contain it. The example of the latter is the signing of the FTA with Pakistan. The removal of Pakistani tariffs on 2,423 products to zero percent will encourage China to buttress her economic position in the Pakistani domestic market, making it difficult for Indian companies to do likewise when a free-trade agreement is reached between Islamabad and New Delhi. China has conducted a similar agreement with Bangladesh in the hope of constricting Indian companies. Indian government split over US relations

Another reason that has persuaded China to enhance its engagement with India is the Congress Party and her allies supplanting BJP as the governing coalition. Distrust of America runs deep in both Congress and her partners. China senses these sentiments and has exploited them to her advantage. For example many of the oil and gas ventures between the two countries flourished under the anti-American Petroleum Minister Mani Shankar Aiyar who was eventually replaced by Manmohan Singh due to US pressure. Still the schisms persist and even the pro-American Manmohan Singh cannot ignore them.

Whereas, China's rapprochement with India is cognisant of anti-American nuance within American-Indian relations, no such differences pervade Pak-US relations. By all accounts Pakistan is a subordinate state to America, and this not only complicates Pakistan's relationship with China, but hinders Beijing from enhancing its ties with Islamabad.

Resurgence of Islam

The resurgence of political Islam across the Muslim world has forced China to explore relations with non-Islamic countries. Since September 11, China has sought to expand security cooperation with Russia, Israel and India as a means of countering political Islam, in particular the re-emergence of the Caliphate. A few years ago Russia and China invited India to discuss this very prospect.

All of these factors have contributed to China's expansion of ties with India. But the eventual outcome of US-China-India-Pakistan relations hinges on three issues: America's ability to extricate itself from Afghanistan and Iraq; Pakistan ability to wrest control of its domestic and foreign policy from America; China's ability to assert itself as a global power.

If the present trends continue then Sino-Pakistan relations will quickly degenerate and Pakistan will be bereft of its only friend in the international arena China.

2 December 2006

Chinese Relationship with Ex USSR Nations

Question: It is noted that the political situation in West Turkistan (Central Asia:-Kyrgyzstan, Uzbekistan, Tajikistan, Kazakhstan and Turkmenistan), is in a volatile state, sometimes we find such and such ruler under the mantle of Russia and after a while he rushes toward America ... and so on, can you clarify the current political situation in these republics?

Answer:

Before getting into the details of the political situation in Central Asia and its volatility, we must be aware of the following matters:

1 - When the Soviet Union disintegrated in 1991, and its former republics seceded, Russia was aware that it is essential to maintain a strong link with these republics, because they are neighboring regions ... essentially she tried to gather them in the so-called "Commonwealth of Independent States (CIS)," but many of that association withdrew from it later whereas some did not enter the association at all, such as the three Baltic states ... after that she used the Shanghai Cooperation Organization (SCO), the Collective Security Treaty Organization (CSTO) and CSTO's Rapid Reaction Force and so on...

Russia also used centers of influence that she established in these republics during the era of the former Soviet Union, amongst whom the most notable are:

A – a demographic change created by the Soviet Union, particularly in the Central Asian Republics, wherein a Russian population was introduced and remained in the republics as "Russia's arm " ...

B – Russian bases, which were spread throughout these republics and which were not all withdrawn. So, some bases remain present in the Central Asian Republics and are centers of power and the frontline for Russia.

C - The nuclear and missile tests fields that were conducted in these republics, and Kazakhstan in particular because of its vast area...

D - Some economic ties with those countries, such as gas and oil pipelines...

2 - Although the disintegration of the Soviet Union produced a near-collapse of the Communist Party and excluded it from ruling, in the Central Asian Republic, the heads of the Communist Party remained the rulers, which means that those who were rulers in the era of the Soviet Union continued in government. The aim of this malicious plan is to allow the governments of these republics to keep fighting Islam and the people who work for it, even after the demise of the Soviet Union, out of fear of the effective spread of Islam within these republics, their unification on the basis of Islam, ruling by Islam and performance of Jihad in His path.

3- The disintegration of the Soviet Union was an opportunity that America did not miss. Central Asia, apart from neighboring Russia, shares an extensive border with China, making it a strategic area for America. Accordingly, America begun to spread its agents, institutions, intelligence and above all, its money, in order to secure a foothold in these republics.

Thus, Central Asia is a vital and strategic interest for both Russia and America, and the conflict between them that had eased has now intensified again. Therefore, it is not surprising that there is continual change in the influence and the type of agency of the rulers of this region, in accordance with the strength of influence available to each competitor:

* As for Russia, it has its former supporting factors: the demographic change that has been mentioned previously, let us call them the "Russian community" in these Republics, as well as their former bases and economic ties and so on...

* As for America, she has generous "carrots" on offer to these Republics, i.e. financial assistance, as well as her proposal to them that Russia is no

longer a major power that they should be fearful of, and her promise of protection...

* This is from the aspect of an intense conflict between Russia and America in the region.

* However, the other aspect is the enmity of the rulers against Islam and the carriers of Islam, a matter which both parties in the conflict agree with.

In the light of these matters, we will review the political scenario in these Republics:

1 - Kyrgyzstan:

We know how Bakiyev came to power in 2005 backed by Russia. He then renewed his presidency in the recent elections of 23/7/2009. Russia's support of him was clear, as was America's dissatisfaction with him. The U.S. Embassy issued a statement in Bishkek saying, "The United States shares the concern expressed by many observers regarding the presidential elections and its results. And that, whilst there were some positive aspects of the voting process, the United States has reservations that the elections in the Kyrgyz Republic did not fulfill many democratic requirements." The statement called for a "strict application of the electoral laws during the entire electoral process in accordance with democratic requirement in the Republic of Kyrgyzstan." (France-Press 2/8/2009). In contrast, the Russians congratulated Bakiyev on his re-election and the Russian President, Dmitry Medvedev, visited Kyrgyzstan in 31/7/2009 and met with him to congratulate him and declare his support, before Bakiyev's formal inauguration for a second presidential term on 2/8/2009. It was announced that the Russian president's visit to Kyrgyzstan came within the context of the summit of the Collective Security Treaty Organization in the Kyrgyz city of Cholponata. It was stated in "Russia Today" on 1/8/2009 that "Russian President Medvedev signed on Saturday, 1/8/2009 in Cholponata in Kyrgyzstan, a document on the development and improvement of post-contractual legal basis of bilateral relations, governing the presence of the Russian formations and the presence of the Kyrgyz-Russian additional unit in this country. The document provides for the establishment of a joint training center for Russian and Kyrgyz military." And it was reported on Russia today, "The two presidents agreed on the drafting and signing a special agreement to establish a military base for the rapid reaction forces in the south of Kyrgyzstan for 49 years with a possible extension for another 25 years." It also stated that, "Bakiyev noted that the agreement must be signed before the first of next November and it will determine the entire Russian military presence in the country."

As for why Bakiyev re-extended the lease for the American Manas airbase, after it was threatened with closure- that does not indicate that Bakiyev distanced himself from Russia and shifted to America. Rather this extension was with the permission of the Russia in order to placate America, so that she will not move her followers in Kyrgyzstan against the regime, for they are able to disturb the regime's "comfort" and thus have an adverse effect on the Russian bases in Kyrgyzstan. And so as to clarify this, we will recap the story of the base from the beginning:

Bakiyev had tried to close the American Manas air base in February 2009. The President of Kyrgyzstan, Kurmanbek Bakiyev, announced from Moscow that he will close the Manas base (Reuters 12/2/2009) and he elaborated further by saying: "Over the past three years I personally raised the issue of increasing the rent for the base with senior U.S. officials. I told them that we shall review the terms of our agreement, the prices have changed and Kyrgyzstan is in a difficult financial situation." He added, "They always respond to us; okay 'fine.' They have done so for years. But how long can we wait, we are a sovereign state and we should demand respect." (Reuters 12/2/2009).

It may understood from this that the problem of the Kyrgyz regime is acquiring funds. It may also understood that the Americans did not care for three years, even though Kyrgyzstan was begging them. Kyrgyzstan's parliament -which is under the control of Bakiyev's party- had adopted a resolution to shut down the American base. And it gave the US 180 days to leave. But before the deadline expired, an agreement between the two parties was announced in mid-July 2009. The U.S. embassy in Bishkek issued a statement regarding the agreement, included "The Government of the United States and the Kyrgyz Republic have agreed in their negotiations for the continued use of the Manas Air Base," (Al-Jazeera 15/7/2009). It was reported that the rent rose to $150 million annually, after it had been 17 million! The truth is it was in the previously it was "17 million basic rent with an additional 133 million as aid, making a total of $150 million annually." Under the new agreement it has become "the basic rent of 60 million with financial assistance of 90 million, making a total of $150 million annually." As such nothing actually changed regarding the rent issue, rather it only termed the financial aid and the non-financial aid which was provided to Kyrgyzstan as "rent," instead of the term "aid," so as to preserve the prestige of Kurmanbek as a president of a country that wants to be respected and so that he shows that the state is respected regarding her sovereignty, as he said!! The New York Times 24/7/2009 has stated something similar to what we have said above about the actions of Bakiyev. It stated, "The agreement signed recently by the governments of Kyrgyzstan and the United States to extend the use of the America Manas air base is only a way to save the prestige of the Kyrgyz government in its reversal of its decision to close the base and to increase the annual rent for the base." Russia was behind this and the new agreement was announced after the meeting between US President Obama and Russian President Medvedev in Russia from 6 to 8/7/2009, when Russia agreed to allow US and NATO supplies to pass through the territory of Russia and her allies. Russia was anxious about its base in Kant, Kyrgyzstan. Her concern was that if she did not settle with America regarding its base, America would work on "color" revolutions, aimed at overthrowing Bakiyev, who protects Russian interests in Kyrgyzstan.

All of this indicates the loyalty of Bakiyev to Russia. Bakiyev's allowing the Americans to continue to use the Manas air base in their operations against the Muslims in Afghanistan is only to satisfy the Americans, so that they do not move to overthrow him, as they did with his predecessor, Askar Akaev. He did so with the consent of the Russians, who want to maintain their presence and influence in Kyrgyzstan, fearing that otherwise America would work on destabilizing him and then overthrowing him.

As for why there is a conflict between Russia and America, it is because of Kyrgyzstan's important strategic location in Central Asia. It border with China extends for 858 kilometers. If America gained Kyrgystan it would become a base for her on the borders of China. Kyrgyzstan is of utmost importance for America in her work against China and the entire region. The Manas base has been of central importance in the war against Muslims in Afghanistan, since 2001 until today, and has a permanent presence of more than 1,000 US troops. The Kyrgyz government does not know anything about what happens in the Manas base, because the agreement states that no inspectors, Kyrgyz observers or anyone else are allowed to enter the base and that there is to be no inspection of any cargo, entering or exiting the US base. The base is far from Kyrgyz control and therefore it is far from the control of the Russians. "Russia Today" stated on 31/7/2009, within the news about Medvedev's visit to Kyrgyzstan and the issue of signing the military agreements with Bakiyev, that, "Kyrgyzstan has an important strategic location, unique in Central Asia and for many years has been marked as the intersection point of the interests of Western countries and Russia." This means that there is a conflict between Russia and the West, led by America within this strategic location. Recently, US General David Petraeus, the commander of US forces, visited three Central Asian Republics, including Kyrgyzstan, the other two being Turkmenistan and Uzbekistan. The Russians reported via the news agency "RIA Novosti" on 20/8/2009 that commented hailed General Petraeus's visit as successful because officials confirmed in the three capitals that they want to increase cooperation with Washington. This visit is just part of the intense American activity in these countries, including Kyrgyzstan, in an attempt to attain and strengthen US presence there. Although the Kyrgyz President Bakiyev did not meet with the US General himself, Petraeus was met by the Kyrgyz Minister of Foreign Affairs. This is despite the fact that Bakiyev is still aware that America is not satisfied with him and has been raising concerns regarding his election. However, he is afraid of American influence upon followers at home and abroad and therefore he wanted to satisfy America. So he concluded the issue of Manas base by allowing America to use the base without changing the basic conditions but only playing with words regard to money to save him and the respect of his country's sovereignty, as he said!

2 - Uzbekistan:

"volatile" is the most apt term to describe the President of Uzbekistan, Karimov. After the disintegration of the Soviet Union, it was quite clear that Karimov started to distance himself from Russia. Russia had formed a joint security organization in 1992 to maintain the cohesion of all the republics of the former Soviet Union, or at least some of them, and then changed its name to the Collective Security Treaty in 2002, similar to the North Atlantic Treaty ... but Karimov has been temperamental towards such organizations. He withdrew from the Collective Security Treaty and joined the GUAM organization which consists of countries of the collapsed Soviet bloc opposed to Russia, such as such as Georgia, Ukraine and Moldova. But he then left the GUAM organization and returned to the Collective Security Treaty, after America and the Western countries demanded to send teams to investigate the Andijan massacre of May 2005, whereas he was supported by Russia and its allies, who have stood by him during the brutal massacres in Andijan and elsewhere ... But then after America closed the subject of massacres and human rights violations, which is tied to US interests, America began contacting him and trying to attract him. Karimov returned to display a suspension of activities with Russians and started to show activity with the Americans and to work with them. The peak of his leaning towards America was when Russia felt that the Collective Security Treaty no longer met her security needs and aspirations of sovereignty and influence. She resorted to what is called the Rapid Reaction Force which entailed a rapid reaction to any threat to Russian influence in the region. But, Uzbekistan stood against it. She did not sign the convention for establishing the Rapid Reaction Force and stood against the deployment of forces in the region of the Collective Security Treaty Organization, which includes Russia, Belarus, Kazakhstan, Kyrgyzstan, Tajikistan, Armenia, and Uzbekistan. The leaders of these countries then decided to establish a rapid reaction force, under another name "rapid deployment," on 4/2/2009. They signed this convention in Moscow on 14/6/2009, but Uzbekistan refrained from signing it, with Karimov providing an excuse that, "this agreement did not specify the tasks of the joint forces." He suggested that the agreement should stipulate that, "The joint forces only launch in order to repel external aggression and each state of the joint forces shall station only its forces only in its territory." (RIA Novosti 26/8/2009). This indicates that Karimov is aware that this force will be controlled by Russia and that Russian troops will be deployed in the countries mentioned in the Collective Security Treaty, including Uzbekistan. And this force could interfere under any circumstances, allowing Russia to interfere in the territory of the members of this organization, because the tasks were not specified. Therefore, Karimov asked that the forces are deployed only when an attack is external to these countries and nothing else. And also that no troops other than the troops of the participating state are deployed in the territory of each state, i.e. to refuse entry to Russian troops within the Uzbek territory in response to any matter that may threaten Russian influence in Uzbekistan and the region.

Thus, Uzbekistan is currently the opposite of Kyrgyzstan, which agreed to this Convention and allowed the Russians to establish a second base on its territory. Uzbekistan did not participate in the recent exercises of the Collective Security Treaty Organization, which ran from 26 August until 15 October 2009. Uzbekistan's behavior is lukewarm such that its membership in this organization is not announced officially. Not only that, but Uzbekistan has objected to the deployment of a second Russian base in Kyrgyzstan on the grounds that it threatens her sovereignty because the base will be deployed near the Uzbek border, in the Fergana Valley. RIA Novosti quoted on 5/8/2009 that Uzbekistan announced in a statement released by the "Gakhon" agency of the Uzbek Ministry of Foreign Affairs on 3.8.2009 that they do not see "the need or feasibility of implementing the plan for the deployment of a Russian military base, in addition to the other Russian base in southern Kyrgyzstan, noting that the deployment of the new base could lead to instability in the region." It was announced in the statement released by the "Gakhon" agency of the Uzbek Ministry of Foreign Affairs that: "the implementation of such projects in a complex area, where the borders of three Central Asian countries meet, may give impetus to acceleration in militarization of the region and fuel confrontation between various forms of nationalism and raise radical forces." (Novosti 3/9/2009). All this indicates that in recent times the Karimov regime in Uzbekistan clearly began moving away from Russia and is closer to America. And the indications of this are:

* on 18.8.2009 during his meeting with US General David Petraeus, in Tashkent, the capital of Uzbekistan, President Karimov said that "Uzbekistan is ready to extend constructive cooperation with the United States on the basis of the principles of mutual respect and equal partnership." (RIA Novosti Russian 18/8/2009). The US General, David Petraeus, in response said that, "I commend the efforts of Uzbekistan in order to support the stability in Afghanistan and the security in the region," which indicates that Karimov has manifested his desire to return to the Americans and be tied to them. The straw that broke the camel's back in the former relationship between Karimov and the American was his refusal

of America's request to allow the US investigators to investigate his massacres in Andijan, which led America to levy sanctions against him. He turned his back upon America, heading back to Russia, his natural support. When the US put the Andijan incident behind her, he returned, seeking America. And recently the US lifted the sanctions against the Karimov regime in Uzbekistan.

* Observing tensions between Uzbekistan and Russia, the US did not miss the opportunity and sought to develop its relations with Uzbekistan. She signed an agreement with Uzbekistan to transport North Atlantic Treaty Organization (NATO) freight from Uzbekistan to Afghanistan. [Source: National Center for Strategic Studies, 04/04/2009]. However, the relations between Uzbekistan and the US administration did not stop there, rather the US administration issued a congratulatory message to Uzbekistan on the occasion of 18th anniversary of its independence. Then Karimov accepted the visit of the US Ambassador in Uzbekistan, Richard Norland. Before that on 18 August, Karimov accepted the visit of the US CENTCOM Chief, General Hal David Petraeus, and they signed a cooperation agreement between the two countries including military programs, training and vocational education.

Thus, Karimov's is temperamental in this respect and his current reality is distancing himself from Russia and drawing closer to America.

3 - Tajikistan:

The political situation in Tajikistan is similar to the political situation in Kyrgyzstan and President Rakhmanov's loyalty is to Russia and he appreciates the protection of his throne. However, he secures American interests so that they do not stir up trouble against him. Americans have many agents in Tajikistan but until now they can not remove Russian influence. Therefore, America is satisfied with achieving her interests ... at least for the foreseeable future.

The stability of the current President, Rakhmonov, in Tajikistan was achieved with the intervention of Russian troops after a civil war, from 1992 until 1997. He was able to arrive at an agreement to hold elections for a five year presidential term and then hold free elections with the movements which were fighting against him, such as the Popular Movement and the Islamic Renaissance Party. But then Rakhmonov increased his first term to seven years. He then held a referendum on amending the constitution to remain in power until the 2020. When unrest broke out in 2001 in reaction to this amendment, Russia helped him to quell the unrest and secured his throne.

Russia under Putin has strengthened its relations with Rakhmonov. Russia managed to establish a second military base in Tajikistan in August 2008, twenty kilometers from the capital Dushanbe, noting that Russia already has a large military base in Tajikistan established in 1943 called Base No. 201. The Russians have also another station "Ooknu" in Tajikistan to monitor the satellites and the ballistic missiles, which Tajikistan approved in June 2008 to grant to Russia for 49 years. Tajikistan is very important for Russia in strategic terms. Therefore, Russia is holding on to the country and trying to maintain its presence there. So, she supports Rakhmonov regime publicly because he secures all these possibilities for Russia in Tajikistan. Russia is trying to tie Tajikistan economically for control and influence. And Rakhmonov appreciates the Russian assistance that secures and strengthens his rule. Rakhmanov engaged his country in the Collective Security Treaty, tabled by Russia, and agreed to participate in the Rapid Reaction Force led by Russia. Many people in Tajikistan are dependent on remittances from their sons who are working in Russia. In fact these are half a million workers within a total population of seven million. And Tajikistan is also a member of the Shanghai Cooperation Organization (SCO) which is convened by Russia with Chinese assistance. Recently Russia and China carried military exercises in Tajikistan on 18/4/2009 under the auspices of the Shanghai Cooperation Organization.

However, like Bakiyev, Rakhmanov tries not to provoke the United States with the consent of Russia. He secures some of their interests, so that the US does not move against him. Whilst allowing Russian companies to undertake projects up to a value of $2.5 billion, he has also allowed American, European, as well as Chinese, companies to carry out projects and business in Tajikistan. Rakhmonov has offered America the use of airports in the country ... And recently, on 20.2.2009, he has also allowed the passage of the American supplies through Tajik territory to Afghanistan, using Tajik Railways. That was announced by the Deputy Commander of United States Transportation Command (USTRANSCOM), Vice Admiral Mark Harnitchek, during his visit to Tajikistan, when he said, "We intend to transport between fifty to two hundred containers a week from Uzbekistan to Tajikistan and then onto Afghanistan. Tajikistan is very important because it is the closest to our bases." (Al-Jazeera 20/2/2009). And all of this is because Rakhmonov aware that America has political forces in Tajikistan that could affect his rule. If he did not bow to American interests in his country, America can move her followers against him intensively and effectively.

It is worth mentioning that there is a somewhat popular political movement in Tajikistan calling for disengagement with Russia and there are forces in the army and in the government calling for the same thing. Rakhmonov is aware of this, therefore he secures United States interests in exchange for her silence. He also is placating the popular sentiment against Russia. This is why he made some public gestures which appear as if he is distancing himself from Russia. He publically called the commander of Tajik Border Guards for the withdrawal of Russian troops from his country. He stopped the broadcast of Russian language channels in Tajikistan and made the Tajik language the official language instead of Russian, even though this action has irked Russia. Yet Rakhmonov is still closer to Russia, as explained previously.

Tajikistan is strategically important due to its neighboring Afghanistan. Its mountains in the southern eastern part are continuous with the mountains of Afghanistan. The length of its shared border with Afghanistan is about 1206 km, whilst it shares a border with China of around 414 kilometers. In this regard by being close to China, it is as important as Kyrgyzstan. Therefore, America will not overlook Tajikistan and is expected to gain her at any available opportunity.

4 - Turkmenistan:

under the former President Saparmurat Niyazov, it was loyal to Russia and most of her policies were directed by Russia. However, the current President, Gurbanguly Berdi Muhamedow, who came to power after Niyazov in December 2006, has implemented a policy which is more open to the West and involves drawing closer to the West in general and America in particular. In November 2007, he hosted a summit between US and European officials over the energy sector, with the directors of BP and Chevron, alongside Russian companies. He wanted to make clear to them that he wants to deal with everyone. This is also what emerged from a number of agreements made with different parties:

* In May 2007, Russia signed an agreement with Turkmenistan and Kazakhstan to build a new pipeline that keeps the gas of Central Asia under the control of her company Gazprom, by monopolizing the export of most of the gas from Turkmenistan. Putin considered this as a victory for Russia, declaring, "This agreement represents a victory for Russia. It allows Russia to buy gas from Turkmenistan at a price less than the market price." (BBC 17/5/2007). The former Turkmen president Niyazov remained president for two decades. He ensured exclusive Russian monopoly over the gas of the country and prevented access to other parties. Therefore, as an outcome

of previous agreements, Russia currently purchases 90% of Turkmen gas, equivalent to about 50 billion cubic meters annually. She buys at a rate of $100 per 1000 cubic meters of gas and sells it to Europe for up to $250 and more than that during winter, up to $345. Whilst at the time of Niyazov, Russia used to buy at $35, until prices were raised to $70 and then to $100, allowing Russia to gain huge profits from the gas of the Muslims in Turkmenistan. Although prices have been increased, Russia still make huge profits on these gas resources.

* In contrast, Muhamedow agreed in principle to the build of a gas pipeline in the Caspian Sea, according to a project supported by the United States which is intended to reduce Europe's dependence on Russian gas supplies. An agreement was recently signed by the Americans and Europeans in Turkey regarding the Nabucco (Nebuchadnezzar) gas pipeline. So, gas will be piped from Turkmenistan to Azerbaijan and then into the Nabucco pipeline, through Turkey and onto Europe. An unnamed US official was quoted by Reuters on 24/4/2009 US official as saying, "Turkmenistan is the other big potential supplier to the Nabucco project which is supported by the European Union. But Turkmenistan needs to make tangible advances regarding implementation."

* And China is active in this region. Chinese President, Hu Jintao, visited Turkmenistan in April 2006 under former President Niyazov, who had a strong relationship and alliance with Russia and China. The Chinese president then promised during the visit to buy 30 billion cubic meters of gas annually from Turkmenistan. China has extended a gas pipeline from the Amu Darya River in the east of Turkmenistan to reach China. It has been recently announced, on 30/8/2009, that China will undertake a $3 billion development of a gas field in Turkmenistan using the PetroChina company. China has loaned Turkmenistan hundreds of millions of dollars to assist her in the development of its industrial ambitions because of Turkmenistan's great wealth. The size of Turkmenistan's gas production in

2006 was 62. 2 billion cubic meters annually. It will rise to 120 billion cubic meters per annum by 2010.

* The America and European incentive to Turkmenistan is that it would sell its own gas directly to Europe at current prices through the Nabucco pipeline, which will be ready for use in 2014. So, the profit will be hers and not Russia's. This is what inclines Turkmenistan to shift to America and the West. Being a small nation, Turkmenistan will not be able to blackmail or cajole Europe as Russia does. Instead, Turkmenistan will be at the mercy of America and Europe after the implementation of the Caspian gas pipeline. Although the Nabucco pipeline will bring gas from several countries, America will have the upper hand when it controls the sources of gas. Turkmenistan has large gas reserves of up to 100 trillion cubic meters and she is the most important and largest gas producer, not just regionally but globally. In addition, Turkmenistan has significant oil reserves, estimated to be as much as 80 billion barrels. Presently, although the oil is currently not extracted in large quantities, its production not exceeding 200,000 barrels a day, they are planning to reach 2 million barrels a day in the future.

Part of the oil supply for America's military equipment in Afghanistan comes from Turkmenistan. Besides the "Trans-Afghanistan" gas pipeline transfers 1,1 billion cubic meters a year from Turkmenistan to Afghanistan. So, Turkmenistan also became important for America in this regard, asides from America's ambition to control all the oil and gas reserves, not just of Turkmenistan, but the entire world, in order to maintain her dominance and control so as to retain her position as the sole global superpower, as well as to reduce or eliminate the impact of other major powers, such as Russia, and achieve huge profits in the energy sector. For this purpose, America has focused on Turkmenistan, which possesses huge oil and gas reserves upon which Russia depends, in order to take it entirely from Russia or control the lion's share of it. So, she will tightly control Turkmenistan through its imports and exports. Consequently, she will supply gas to Europe instead of Russia, thereby keeping Europe at her mercy and under her hegemony, whilst both weakening Russia's standing and her alliance with Europe. The current allure of Turkmenistan lies in the struggle over her gas wealth, though in the future her oil will play the major role in the struggle.

Despite all of this, Turkmenistan still has great economic ties with Russia that she has not been able to remove as yet. The United States hovers over her to seize her and take her out of this sphere of Russian influence. Russia is aware of this and so when Turkmenistan called for a raise in gas prices to Russia, Russia responded immediately out of fear that Turkmenistan may move in a direction other than dealing with her, turning to American and Western assistance against Russia. The Nabucco project will distance Russia from Turkmenistan's gas supply to Europe, taking Turkmenistan out of the sphere of Russian influence. It should be noted that Turkmenistan is neither a member of the Collective Security Treaty Organization nor the Rapid Reaction Force nor the Shanghai Cooperation Organization and there is no Russian military base in Turkmenistan. Turkmenistan is a subject of attention for Russia, America and the West, and to some extent by China, primarily from an economic aspect, due to her vast oil and gas wealth

5 - Kazakhstan:

Kazakhstan is the largest Central Asian Republic with an area of 2. 7 million square km, although the population is low considering the area, estimated at 15 to 17 million. It was important for Russia in that nuclear tests were conducted there. In fact, Russia has conducted around five hundred nuclear tests at the Semipalatinsk Test Site, Kazakhstan. On 29/9/2009, Kazakh President Nursultan Nazarbayev signed for closure of the test site. Kazakhstan agreed to a ban on nuclear testing in 24/9/2009. America has worked to strengthen its relationship due to Kazakhstan's geo-strategic importance and oil and gas wealth. The oil wealth is estimated at 100 billion barrels. Currently, she produces more than one million barrels a day and production is expected to rise in 2015 to 2.5 million barrels per day. The gas reserves total approximately 150 trillion cubic meters, which makes the

Western colonial powers led by America drool over this wealth and compels them to extend their influence within this large, wealthy Islamic country. Therefore, Kazakhstan's link to America became strong and the Kazakh president granted US companies rights to invest in oil, gas and other sectors such that American companies became the main investors in the country's oil and gas. Dick Cheney, who later was to become US Vice-President, worked in the mid-nineties of the last century in the advisory board for Kazakhstan oil and struck deals for American companies, including a deal in favor of Chevron, in which Condoleezza Rice was working in management at the time. The relationship culminated with the June 2006 visit by Kazakh President Nazarbayev to America to meet President George W. Bush. It was stated in the joint statement they issued, "The partnership between the two countries in the energy field will help American companies to explore the large reserves of oil and gas in Kazakhstan and the Caspian region." (BBC. 30/6/2006).

Kazakhstan approved in February 2009 permission for America to transport equipment and supplies by road, through the Kazakh territory to the US military and NATO forces that are fighting Muslims in Afghanistan. The Russian Chief of Staff, Nicolas Makarov, at the end of last year revealed, "schemes of Washington for the establishment of US military bases in Uzbekistan and Kazakhstan." ("Middle East" 18/12/2009). She has shares a long border with Russia of 6846 km, and it shares a border of 1533 km with China. It has the longest coast on the Caspian Sea, with a length of 1894 km. As such it has strategic and economic importance for America. It has been engaged in a Peace Partnership with NATO. It is considered the United States' biggest ally in Central Asia.

In addition, it is one of the states bordering the Caspian Sea. It is rich in fish, particularly sturgeon fish (caviar fish) of which it produces $400 million worth annually for Russia. It contains huge oil reserves of 200 billion barrels and gas reserves of 600 trillion cubic meters, over which the Western states and America drool. This closed sea is a strategic basin with oil and gas economic riches.

However, Russia has centers of influence in Kazakhstan and has a Russian space launch site there. Therefore Russia has strong ties with it. Russia has re-settled so many Russians there that it has the highest percentage of Russians in any Central Asian Republic, where the percentage has risen from 30% to 40%. The impact is that their nationalist and Orthodox religious ties remain with their native Russia, though the highest percentage is of Muslims at more than 60%.

Recently, Kazakhstan has shown a rapprochement with Russia, a matter to which Russia attaches a high priority as well. Russia made Kazakhstan alongside China as one of the founders of SCO. Kazakhstan is a member of the Commonwealth of Independent States, the Collective Security Treaty Organization led by Russia and the Eurasia economic grouping which was established in 2000 ... She signed to participate in the Rapid Reaction Force whose inception was announced by Russia. China is also working to strengthen ties and has extended terms for a 1240km oil pipeline from Kazakhstan to provide for China's growing oil needs.

Thus, Nazarbayev wants to keep his relationship with Russia and China strong. He expressed his policy once by saying, "If we talked about projects to circumvent the East or the West I answer that we and Turkmenistan have a pragmatic approach" (Russian Interfax 17/5/2007). This means that he sets his policy according to the dictates of reality and immediate interest. Therefore, despite his alliance with America which amounts to close ties and despite what has been leaked recently that the US has plans to establish military bases as well as granting of the Americans the lion's share in oil and gas reserve investment ... in spite of all that, Nazarbayev does not want to disrupt strong relations with Russia so that his regime is not threatened.

In summary, Russia is trying to maintain and strengthen its influence in the Central Asian Republics using various ways and means, whether through regional treaties such as the Commonwealth of Independent States which was established by Russia after the collapse of the former Soviet Union, the Collective Security Treaty, the Rapid Reaction Force or through bilateral treaties and agreements with each state separately and establishing military bases in each and every one of them, so as to strengthen its influence in these countries and to prevent them from slipping out of her hands. She is also leaning on China regionally and internationally through what is known as the Shanghai Treaty Organization, as well as engaging China in the Central Asian Republics. This is all asides from treaties and economic projects ... and the other centers of influence that were set up by the former Soviet Union...

Also, America uses financial aid as a temptation for the Central Asian Republics, in addition to drawing the attention of these states to her strong followers which can stir up unrest within them ... as such she is using the carrot and the stick. She is also working on belittling Russia before the eyes of the Central Asian Republics and other countries in the Caucasus and Eastern Europe, so that none shall fear her and she even encourages them to revolt and escape from her control. US Vice President, Joe Biden, said after his tour in Georgia and Ukraine, "Russia is nothing more than a junior partner of the United States after the loss of her past strategic role." And he said, "The weakness of the Russian economy will compel Moscow to make concessions to the West, in particular the abandonment of attempts to dominate the former Soviet states, and to agree to reduce its nuclear capabilities." (Wall Street Journal 26/7/2009) and this explains the stance of the Central Asian regimes in Central Asia. They recognize the Russian weakness before the Americans, and so not only try to please the Americans, they try to draw close to America.

And the result of this is a volatile conflict in Central Asia, the political reality of which can be described briefly as follows:

Kyrgyzstan and Tajikistan are the principal states that are loyal to Russia, whilst assuring American interests so as not to provoke America by standing in her way, in order to preserve the stability of the political situation in the two countries, which can be disturbed if America moved its followers in both countries strongly and actively.

Uzbekistan is currently leaning in favor of America, taking into account the volatile mood of Karimov.

As in Turkmenistan and Kazakhstan, they are the arena of a contest, politically and economically with America and Russia and to some extent with China economically.

But what is really painful is that all the conflicting parties and competitors, as well as the local rulers, are fighting Islam and its workers and they all abuse the wealth of the Muslims of Central Asia. So the enemies of Islam become rich from Central Asia, whilst the general masses in Central Asia live a miserable existence.

Central Asia has an important location and its enormous wealth will return to the Muslims, inshAllah, when their Khilafah will be established at the hands of the workers for Islam, and that day is not far away from us, inshAllah. And then the believers will rejoice in Allah's victory.

29 Ramadan 1430 H

19 September 2009 CE

Uncharted Strait: China-Taiwan Relations

Question: On January 29th, 2010, the Obama administration announced that the US Congress has been informed of its plan to sell 6.40 billion dolloars of weapons to Taiwan which include Black Hawk helicopters, Patriot Advanced Capability-3 missiles, mine hunter ships and information technology for F-16 fighter aircrafts.

What does the US gain by this deal with Taiwan? How will it tackle its relationship with China which have relatively improved since the economic crisis, and moreover there were expectatations of improvements in the relations especially after Obama having taken over the presidency and visited China in December, 2009? Does Taiwan still matterto it after the US de-recognised it as representing China? Or are there other motives behind the scene? Please clarify, may Allah reward you.

Answer:

Yes, as you have mentioned in the question, the Obama administration has on 29.01.2010 informed the US Congress of its plan to sell 6.40 billion US $ worth of arms to Taiwan that includes Black Hawk helicopters, Patriot Advanced Capability-3 missiles, mine hunter ships and information technology for F-16 fighter aircrafts...

1. As a result of this, the Chinese are very upset and fuming, the Chinese Vice Minister for External Affairs He Yafei expressed his country's strong reaction and issued a statement warning that this deal to sell US arms to Taiwan "It will be unavoidable that co-operation between China and the United States over important international and regional issues will also be affected." He added: "This new American plan to sell arms to Taiwan which is an inseparable part of China constitutes gross intervention in the internal affairs and exposes the national security of China to great danger and jeopardise efforts towards a peaceful re-unification of the country." The US

ambassador to Beijing was called and serious protest was conveyed to him. [Chinese News Agency Xin Hua: 30.01.21010].

After this, the Chinese Foreign Minister Yang Jiechi termed his country's reaction over US arms sale to Taiwan as "very reasonable", he said:" "We approached the U.S. side very seriously on many occasions. Yet the U.S. went ahead with the deal worth 6.4 billion US$." He added:"This plan grossly violates the 3 joint communiqués between the US and China, especially the 17th August communiqué."The American decision to sell more weapons to Taiwan "constitutes a gross intervention into China's internal affairs, seriously endangers China's national security and harms China's peaceful reunification efforts," Mr. He said in the ministry's statement. He demanded that the US immedeately cancel the erroneous decision with regard to the arms deal and respect China's vital interests as well as respect the US obligation to support peaceful development of relations across the Taiwan straits. [Xin Hua: 30.01.21010]. The Chinese foreign ministry as well as the foreign relations committee of the Chinese Peoples Congress have issued similar and strong statements expressing their protest over the US arms deal with Taiwan. In addition to this China has taken certain steps protesting the same, the foreign ministry issued a statement saying: "China has decided to partially freeze the exchange programme between the armed forces of the two countries as well as high-level consultation on strategic security, arms control and non-proliferation issues which were originally scheduled to be held shortly. "The statement further said:" China will impose sanctions on American companies involved in the arms sale to Taiwan." The statement also said that "Sino-US cooperation in regional and greater international affairs will certainly be affected because of this deal." [Xin Hua: 30.01.21010].

2. On the other hand the Chinese reactions and their intensity has been very visible while the US response over the Chinese reactions was lukewarm and uncaring with no senior US administration official speaking on the subject with exception of the US State Department's spokeswoman Laura Tischler

saying: " "Such sales contribute to maintaining security and stability across the Taiwan Strait," She further remarked that such arms sale are consistent with the One China policy of the United States and its Taiwan Relation Act. The sale, she said is also in line with the 3 pact that guide the US-China relations. [Reuters: 30.01.2010].

But it may be mentioned that the US action actually violates the three communiques especially the 17th August Communique wherein the US is committed to refrain from taking any action to implement long-term policies for arms sale to Taiwan and is required to work to gradually reduce arms sale to the Island!

3. The American action is not simply incidental, nor is it a merely a matter of trade profit through arms sale to Taiwan, it is intended to put pressure on China and force it into agreeing with the US in various matters including upward revaluation of the Chinese currency against the US dollar and opther trade issues as well as the cencorship of the US electonic serach engine "Google" in which the United States has directly been involved.

4. Moreover due to America's shaken standing after the financial crisis as well as its problems in Iraq and Afghanistan, China is begining to emerge from its own region into the international political arena; therefore the US is trying to create an effective problem within the vicinity of China, thus engaging it there and further heating up the already tense situation. On the other hand the US wants to send the message to China that the US is strong and its writ runs globally. This is also the message for the other big nations of the world at large.

5. As for Taiwan importance to the US, it amounts to nothing in comparison with Amrica's interest that it can acheive with China. In 1979 the US had withdrawn its recognition to Taiwan as being representative of the Chinese people. Obama has added other features to please the Chinese since coming to power apart from the broad smiles he gave to them during his last visit in Decmber 2009 when he welcomed China's emergence into an

international role. Obama expressed his intentions to strengthen and devlop relations with China including military relations...This is because the US needs China in many issues whether financial, trade or foreign policy...

. All this indicates that it is not possible for the US to sacrifice its relations with China neither for a mere 6.40 billion US dollars nor for the sake of Taiwan which amounts to nothing on the global political map which the US has alrady forsaken as being reprensentative of the Chinese people...

Thus the tensions with China will not reach beyond a measured point especially because the US is convinced that the Chinese reactions will not spell a breaking point in their bilateral relations, as a US official recently commented:"The Chinese reactions are temporary."

16th Safar, 1431 A.H

1st February 2010 C.E

China-India Relationship and The China-South Korea-Japan trilateral deal

Question:

On 16 December 2010, the media reported two matters for long-term consideration: the first being the visit of the Prime Minister of China to India with a large trade delegation, of around 300 business men. This visit has been accompanied with unusual warmth. The second matter is that of a trilateral deal between South Korea, China and Japan to establish a co-operative secretariat between the three countries. This is along with cooling of tensions between the two Koreas , with respect to mutual threat between the US and South Korea on one side and North Korea on the other, with tacit support from China to North Korea . What is the significant of these happenings?

Answer:

To answer this question, we review the following:

1- Since the 1960s America has feared the emergence of China as a world power and has sought to restrict China 's ambitions to regional matters. America has used a variety of issues to contain China 's sphere of influence, and to keep her leadership preoccupied with parochial problems. America has persistently exploited the issue of Taiwan , North Korea , autonomy for Tibet , poor treatment of Chinese minorities (East Turkistan, Falun Gong etc.) and interference in bilateral disputes between China and Japan over islands as a means of lighting fires around China 's borders. Additionally, America has a string of bases stretching from Afghanistan , Central Asia, and Pakistan to the Asian Pacific rim that includes the Korean peninsula, Japan…. The aim of these military bases is to ensnare China and prevent her from projecting military power.

2- Notwithstanding efforts to curb China's military expansion, America has also aggressively sought to build India's civil and military capabilities to offset China . Speaking before a joint sitting of Indian parliament Obama said, "I stand before you today because I am convinced that the interests of the United States - and the interests we share with India - are best advanced in partnership…United States not only welcomes India as a global power. We fervently support it. Promoting shared prosperity, preserving peace and security, strengthening democratic governance and human rights — these are the responsibilities of leadership. As global partners this is the leadership United States and India can offer in the 21st century…With my visit, we are now ready to begin implementing our civil nuclear agreement...We need to forge partnerships in high-tech sectors like defense and civil space." (US supports India as global power, the Indian Online, Nov 8 2010). It is noteworthy that India on September 29th 2010 sent 4 personnel from the Indian army, air force and navy to train with the U.S. 's 31st Marine Expeditionary Unit at the latter's base in Okinawa in the East China Sea during 2010.

China has vigorously reacted to such military exercises. In late September China 's Rear Admiral Yin Zhuo warned that, "A series of military drills initiated by the US and China 's neighboring countries showed that the US wants to increase its military presence in Asia . The purpose of these military drills launched by the US is to target multiple countries including China , Russia and North Korea and to build up strategic ties with its allied countries like Japan and South Korea." (Global Times, September 26, 2010).

3- A familiar pattern has prevailed ever since the six-party talks were instigated in 2003 to reign in North Korea 's nuclear ambitions. This consists of America making certain demands during the six-party talks and when North Korea is close to meeting the demands, America reneges on its commitments. Furthermore, America has skillfully portrayed North Korea , with China as its main backer, as the guilty party during the fall out from the failed talks. For instance in 2007 the US announced that it would release $25million dollars of North Korea's frozen money, in return for Pyongyang to freeze its Yongbyon nuclear reactor and readmit IAEA inspectors. However, the US reneged on its promise and released the money very late, such that the transaction could not be completed on time. North Korea promptly withdrew from the six-party talks. Frustrated by numerous obstacles placed by the US , North Korea eventually withdrew from the talks in 2009 and adopted a more belligerent posture in an effort to restart negotiations on more favorable terms. The aggressive stance adopted by North Korea included expulsion of IAEA inspectors, announcing plans to resume enrichment, detonating a nuclear devise underground in May 2009, clashing with South Korea's Navy and the recent attack on a South Korean island.

4- The American response via the deployment of aircraft carriers, military exercises and convening talks minus, China and North Korea, has been to pressurize China to take a more forceful stance against its surrogate state. Admiral Mike Mullen, US Chairman of Joint Chiefs of Staff, remarked on 8 December 2010 that he wished the Chinese would be more helpful, saying, "The Chinese have enormous influence over the North, influence that no other nation on earth enjoys. And yet, despite a shared interest in reducing tensions, they appear unwilling to use it," he said. It is interesting to note that in the immediate aftermath of the attack, China swiftly called for the resumption of the six-party talks, which was rejected by America. And lately, China has come out to publicly defend North Korea against America 's intrusion in the region! This means that America wants to keep tensions raised and to present China and North Korea as if they were the source of tension and thus antagonize the countries of the region against them, but without reaching to the brink of war, because international and regional circumstances do not allow her to do so as America is busy in Iraq and Afghanistan.

5- In light of all this, we can say that the current Chinese measures, the signing of an accord by China Japan and South Korea on 16 December 2010 for establishing a tripartite cooperative secretariat in Seoul next year, as published by China on its network (Arabic.china.org.cn) Xinhua News Agency or what was published in multiple media sources, including this site, regarding the Chinese Prime Minister's visit to India ... All of these measures are to undermine America's efforts to isolate China from its neighbors and portray China as the aggressive party. South Korea and Japan are most pro-American and any close tie between them and China undermines America 's exploitation of them against China. Also, India has been, and continues to be, one of the weapons that America exploits to trigger permanent tension betweens India and China, founded upon perennial disputes between them. Therefore China 's closeness to India is to extinguish the flames of tension that America is trying to maintain between China and India.

It is expected that China has scored a point in its favor in countering America. That is if China exploits its visit to India and its agreement with Japan and South Korea well. And also if she did not fall into a trap of deception sprung by Japan and South Korea but backed by America.

21st of Muharram 1432 AH
17 December 2010 CE

China - Japan Relations

Question:

U.S. Defense Secretary during his visit to Japan on 16-17/9/2012 said that "this dispute between China and Japan on the subject of the islands can intensify" (A.P. News Agency 17/9/2012) and then added "I am worried because when these countries start provoking one another on these disputed islands, it would enhance the possibility of making the wrong decision from one side or the other, which on its part could lead to violence and result in conflict" (the above source). The current development came to the fore in the wake of the announcement made by Japan on 11/9/2012 that she bought the three islands from a Japanese family in an archipelago of the East China Sea, thus she claims their ownership and calls them Senkaku. This scenario triggered tension between them and China who claims that these islands belong to them and she calls them Diaoyu. China sent two warships towards these islands…

So the question is: why did Japan take this step at this juncture? Does America have a role in this conflict? Is it possible that the situation will drive them to the outbreak of war or is it a storm which will calm down?

Answer:

Answer to the question gets clarified by reviewing the following matters:

1- China claims that these three islands are from among the five main islands owned by her and were captured by Japan in the war that took place between them during 1894 and 1895. The Americans took control of them in World War II after they defeated the Japanese. They (Americans) annexed the administration of these islands to the Japanese island of Oukinao which they also occupied in the same war and established therein a large U.S. base. The

America, however, handed over these islands to the Japanese in 1972 by handing over them to a Japanese family and then these islands were bought by another Japanese family who were controlling them since the nineties of the nineteenth century. The area of all these islands in the archipelago is about 6.2 km, including the rocks surrounded by the sea water. These islands are uninhabited but they are of strategic importance in the East China Sea. They are close to the routes of maritime navigation and their waters are replete with fish wealth. Also there are reports about the possibility that they may have large reserves of oil and gas.

The issue of these islands has been raised between the two countries several times, the last of which was in the year 2010 when a similar tension arose.

2- The United States officially informed Japan on 29/06/2012 that they want to deploy "12" Osprey aircrafts in the U.S. Futenma base in the Japanese island of Oukinao and that the deployment of these aircrafts will be at the end of the ongoing month (ASHA - Musrs – scene - masress almashhad 1.7.2012) and U.S. forces announced that one of these aircrafts will begin its trip on 21/9/2012 (Arabic News CN World 20.9.2012). All this came in an atmosphere witnessing Japanese protests against the American presence, which was started to be looked at unpleasantly, with some of them even demanding the departure of the Americans from their country as there are still 47 thousand U.S. troops by virtue of a bilateral security treaty signed in 1960 with the Government of Japan under the U.S. occupation. This is an American method which she has resorted to in order to change the form of her occupation and keep her influence in the country occupied by her as she did in Iraq when she held the U.S. security treaty with the Maliki government in 2008 under American official occupation as well as the American strategic security agreement with the Government of Afghanistan, which was signed a few month ago under the patronage of ongoing American occupation.

In such atmosphere of Japanese dissatisfaction with the largely American presence in their country, America announces the deployment of aircrafts! Of course, such announcement will intensify the opposition by the Japanese... So America deemed it appropriate that creating an atmosphere of provocation with China and manifestation, that the war with China is approaching, will make the Japanese accept the deployment of these aircrafts and will mitigate their protests against the American presence, on the pretext that the U.S. will support Japan in the face of China! That's why and in agreement with the Japanese government closely related to U.S. policy was raised the issue of the islands that they belong to Japan while they are disputed between the two. This scenario provoked China and created an atmosphere of misleading clash with her and that the war may erupt. And this is what pacified the Japanese opposition to the American presence in their country considering that they would lend a helping hand to them in the face of China.

3- Therefore, raising the issue of the islands this time, after the announcement to deploy the aircrafts, is a deliberate step by the Government of Japan based on the U.S. plan to provoke the Chinese until the tension between Japan and China becomes apparent so that the Japanese are terrified by China and surrender to the American plans to be implemented in their region. Therefore the statements by U.S. officials indicate the forthcoming confrontation or that they are prelude to confrontation! U.S. Defense Secretary during his visit to Japan said on 16-17/9/2012 "this dispute between the two can intensify" (A.P. News Agency 17/9/2012) and then added "I am worried because when these countries start provoking one another on these disputed islands, it would enhance the possibility of making the wrong decision from one side or the other, which on its part could lead to violence and result in conflict" (the above source). He called on "the two sides to equanimity and self-control". U.S. Defense Secretary describes the issue as if a war is about to occur between the two countries for the sake of the American goals. He reminded Japan of the security pacts between his country and Japan to show that America is ready to stand by Japan and said "we honor our commitments related to the treaties existing for a long time and will not change" (the above source). All these escalations are happening at a time when the US Defense Secretary is focusing in his talks with the Japanese government on the US Plans to deploy 12 Osprey aircrafts in the U.S. base in the Japanese island of Oukinao amid strong opposition from the residents of the South Island as reported French News Agency on 16/9/2012.

4- The Chinese reaction was emotional and the mass demonstration were allowed to roam through the streets of her cities to protest against the Japanese step towards these islands that are officially not controlled by the Japanese state. But when it announced the purchase of three of them from the Japanese family to be owned by the Japanese state, the sovereignty of these islands officially came under the Japanese state and it was considered as if these islands were again annexed by Japan. This Japanese action provoked China who moved some of her ships that guard her territorial waters in the East China Sea toward these islands. The Prime Minister of China Wen Jiabao being impressed and touched by the Chinese emotions said: "the era of humiliating the Chinese has gone irrevocably" (A.P. News Agency 17/9/2012). The Chinese still remember the humiliation that they suffered from at the hands of the Japanese, whether it is in the war that broke out between them in the nineties of the nineteenth century or it is the direct Japanese occupation of China in the thirties of the twentieth century which lasted until Japan's defeat in World War II by America. So they went out of Chinese control and then were left for Americans. The complication of defeat and humiliation that afflicted the Chinese at the hands of the Japanese is still a factor of provocation among them. So the Chinese getting agitated by such an issue is very easy.

5- Thus, America hit two birds with one stone by pushing Japan to claim the islands… on the one hand the atmosphere became strained between

China and Japan so that Japan feel compelled to have the American presence, which can be easily acceptable to the Japanese. On the other hand, America wants to keep China always busy with tense regional issues, thus preventing China from any aspirations towards any global state policy except within the limits of its territory. America continues in her plans aimed at restraining China and putting an end to China's plans to strengthen its regional position in order to reach the global status, particularly towards America. Thus, the U.S. plan in the regional areas of China is to achieve this goal. America has already announced her plans to strengthen her presence in Asia/ Pacific Ocean as part of a new strategy when her defense secretary Leon Panetta announced on 01/06/2012 this strategy of his country in Asia/ Pacific Ocean regarding sending six aircrafts carriers and deploying 60% of its warships in this region over the coming years until 2020. Thus America is working towards igniting all the conflicts in the face of China: in the region of the East China Sea as happened with Japan and in the South China Sea as there is tension between China and the Philippines over the islands and the fishing, and also there is dispute between China and Vietnam over the islands where the Chinese stood up and expelled the Vietnamese in 1988. All this is aroused to keep China busy in these two regions!

America also stands behind these countries in the two regions with the exception of North Korea, and incites them against China so that the latter, as we said above, is made busy in her own region and cannot be in a position to go beyond this territory, especially in view of the fact that America has full control over many of these countries such as South Korea in the East China Sea, the Philippines in the South China Sea, where there are U.S. bases as well as Indonesia subordinate to U.S. policy and then Japan which is also in the American orbit.

6- This is the reality about America's role in this matter and triggering the issue of the islands at this time. As for the question that this provocation will reach to the outbreak of war between China and Japan over the islands, it is unlikely at least in the foreseeable future because there are islands larger and more important than these such as the island of Taiwan, formerly known as Formosa and for which China did not ignite a war considering that America is agreed with her that she would work to peacefully bring them back to China. Then there is a conflict with the Philippines, Vietnam and others on islands located in the South China Sea, without getting into war with them. Otherwise, she will open upon herself a door which she cannot close! China will never sacrifice its large interests with Japan because of these islands, for the reason that the volume of trade between them is about $ 300 billion a year and the Japanese companies operating in China employ more than 20 million Chinese workers. In addition, China is working to take advantage of Japanese technology and expertise and therefore it is not in China's interest to ignite a war with Japan for these islands. The Chinese Defense Minister Liang Gwaungla said in his meeting with U.S. Defense Secretary on 18/9/2012 while answering to a question by the journalists as to whether Beijing intends to resort to force, he said that "we still hope to have a peaceful and negotiated solution", (A.P. News Agency 18/9/2012) which indicates that it is unlikely on the part of China to ignite a war with Japan for these islands.

7- If China remains preoccupied with her territorial issues, America could succeed in expelling China from international politics. However it is true that China is effectively threatening the U.S. policy worldwide and creates problems to her, which threaten the latter's interests i.e. China applies the policy of effective threat to the U.S. policy in every region of the world and therefore it is easy for China to have effective influence in her regional domain, especially in the two regions of East and South China Sea.

However, the noticeable prospects in the Chinese policy are that it is still misled by the notion that her effective interference in the international politics is not in her best interest and so she only takes care of her regional areas… and is not aware of the fact that she will never be able to control her regions if she does not have global political aspirations of creating problems for America in order to compel the latter to lessen the harassment of China in its territory. Unless China pursues this policy, she will remain at a standstill and America will continue to create regional tension for her one after the other.

After all, perhaps the history is repeating itself wholly or partially! The Khilaafah, Allah willing, will be established and its international political actions "prior to its military actions "in expelling the West and America from the Islamic region, will be an example to be copied and followed by China in expelling the American influence from around China. Thus the political actions by the Khilaafah will indirectly realize the security to China as the Khilaafah directly achieved security to China in the past. The Chinese and Islamic sources mention that the Chinese state requested the Islamic Khilaafah state at the time of Abbasid Khalifaah Abu Jafar Al-Mansur to assist her in quelling the unrest and chaos occurred in China in 756 CE and engulfed the country. The Khalifah sent a force consisting of 4 thousand Muslim soldiers and thus the matter got stabilized in China and they brought the security for the people of the country. The Chinese became highly impressed by the characters, good behaviors and demeanors of the Muslim soldiers and requested them to stay with them and hence those Muslims soldiers stayed there in their capacity as the Daw'ah carriers, spreading the Deen of Islam, its guidance and light among the people of China. Among their grandsons today are the Muslims of East Turkestan who are currently being oppressed by China instead of reciprocating the favor to them!! Will China get aware of this matter and end its occupation of Turkestan without denying the favor done to her by the Khilaafah in the past?!

4th Dhul Qa'dah 1433 AH
20th September 2012 CE

Chapter 3

Chinese Economy

The Global Economic Crisis & China's response to it

Question:

Where does the global economic crisis currently stand, which began in the USA and engulfed Europe and then the world?

Answer:

To shed light on this subject, we will mention the following:

1. The collapse of the real estate market in the US spread across the world resulting in the collapse of many banks, which lead to unprecedented government intervention to halt global economic collapse. The result however, was what is now called the Great Recession, the worst since the Great Depression in 1929. The global financial crisis brought to light the fact that the boom of the preceding decade was in reality driven by debt; and after five years the world's largest economies continue in their failure to resolve this.

2. United action was attempted by the world's largest economies in order to coordinate a resolution to the crisis. This was argued on the basis that the global economy is interlinked due to the effects of globalisation. Thus, a collective and global approach would be in the world's best interests. This unified approach did not last long as economic nationalism - where each country fights for its own survival spread, where each nation expected other nations to fund a global reserve. Various meetings and conferences of the G20 agreed different types of bailout funds to help grieved economies, how this was to be funded led to most of the bailouts to never move forward from the paper they were written on. This was due to the concept

of economic nationalism of the super-powers. "The Economist" highlighted in 2010, *"But the re-emergence of a spectre from the darkest period of modern history requires a different response, even serious. Economic nationalism that strives to save jobs and capital at home turned the economic crisis into a political one and threatened the world with depression. If it is not buried again forthwith, the consequences will be dire."*

3.   Stark exchanges between the Germans and the Americans have taken place on the best route for the future of the global economy. Angela Merkel, along with the majority of the other countries suggested that the unsustainable growth model of the US, fuelled by the cheap credit and debit/loans, from the governments' perspective using funds as stimulus for growth is obsolete. The European approach has manifested in the need to control the national deficit through austerity measures. Austerity measures are typically taken if there is a threat that a government cannot honour its debt liabilities. This is a very specific objective and different to economic growth. With the threat to the credit ratings of most of the world's largest economies, many have resorted to austerity i.e. reducing the government deficit to please the financial markets. The problem with the austerity approach is that such a policy is not actually geared towards growth, which would create jobs and income for society, and accordingly lead to overall economic growth, but towards cutting the government debt.

4.   The US approach of seeking to stimulate the growth has fared no better. This is because stimulus requires increasing government spending using funds borrowed primarily from abroad in the case of the US from countries such as China, or funds simply created by central banks literally by entering digits into a computer. Any stimulus was always a high-octane boost and a temporary measure. They are designed to kick-start stalled economies, not to fuel

sustained economic growth. The growth that has been achieved is really the inflated results of stimulus measures achieving their intended effect to be temporary. Hence stimulus just props up government and service industry jobs which die off when the stimulus ends, leaving an economy in much the state it was when the stimulus started.

5. Western governments also resorted to Quantitative Easing (QE), a new development which was an electronic method of printing money. This unconventional policy was used by central banks (governments) to stimulate the national economy when conventional policy had failed. Accordingly, central banks started to implement the so-called Quantitative Easing (QE) through buying financial assets, such as bonds in order to inject a pre-determined quantity of money into the economy. This is achieved by purchasing financial assets from banks with new electronically created money. This action increased the reserves of banks. However, the global economy at the start of 2013 is not better than it was at the start of 2012. Rather the great recession has eaten away some of the States that tried to avoid falling into the recession. Reports have emerged as soon as 2013 began about the possibility of Britain going into a triple dip recession, due to its debt burden going into the trillions Thus, the QE approach ended up in reality with no effective result. After 5 years of economic crisis, the global economy is still reeling and with unemployment constantly increasing social chaos has already begun in Europe. All attempts to solve the crisis have not dealt with debt fuelled growth, whilst debt caused the problem more debt was thrown at it, Western governments attempted to treat the patient with the disease itself

6. Finally, there are three possibilities that may eventually lead to economic recovery; we mention them from the least to the best:

First: The first is the double-dip recession turns into a depression, prices hit rock bottom and this leads to property, loans and commodity prices being seen as cheap and this kick starts economic growth as such assets are then purchased. This is a weak possibility because the Capitalist economy is primarily based on loans and interest (riba) that results from them. The decline of loans prices (riba) do not live long as long as capitalist economy continues.

Second: The second possibility is China bails out the West. China's vast trade and financial surpluses are causally linked to the unsustainably large debts of the US, UK and a swathe of the Eurozone. It would be in their interests to bail out the West. This would also mean the Western world will have to accept Chinese global leadership. Here the issue is not whether the West will accept such a bailout but rather will China pursue such a policy.

Third: The Khilafah State shines on the world, and the Islamic economic system starts to be implemented. Then, not only will the Muslims benefit, but rather all the world that will deal with it. This would make such global crises disappear or bring it under control.

02 Rabii I 1434 AH
14 January 2013 CE

Chinese Economic Situation

Question:

On Friday 09/06/2013 the G-20 Economic Conference was concluded in St .Petersburg with the adoption of the final statement. The statement said , as quoted by Reuters News Agency on 09/06/2013, "that the global economy is getting better..." Reuters also quoted Andre Bockarev ,Director of the Department of Finances in the Russian Ministry of Finance, who participated in the drafting of the final statement of the G-20 : "The most difficult and longest discussion was the assessment of the global economy". Recently data appeared indicating this improvement, and the European Union spread that its economy began to grow albeit slightly. The United States said that its economy grew by 1% in 2013, and China published that its economy grew this year until the month of July 2013 by more than 7%.

Is the global economy really improving and has the economic crisis eased, during the past six years since its outbreak in America in 2007? In case the economy has not improved, how then were these data and figures announced?

Answer:

We will review the economic reality of the economically most influential countries in the world, which are the United States, the European Union and China, since the economy of these three countries represent more than 50% of the global economy, and because of the economic crisis being closely linked to the capitalist system adopted by the United States and the European Union. Therefore they carry the driving impact on the crisis, while China's role during the crisis was to overcome it, thus playing a reactionary role rather than a progressive one, as we will demonstrate later. For your information, the U.S. economy alone approaches the economies of China, Japan and Germany combined, the three largest economic powers in the world that come after the U.S. economy respectively. The total size of the U.S. economy in the year 2012 amounted to $15.7 trillion, which represents 22% of the global economy .The Chinese economy reached $8.2 trillion, while the Japanese and the German economy have reached the $5.9 trillion and $3.4 trillion respectively according to the World Bank and the Organization for Economic Cooperation and Development. Because of the large size of the U.S. economy, America's economic crisis that resulted from the collapse of the mortgage market in America spread to the world. Accordingly we will focus the research on the economy of these three most influential countries in the global economy, and because the most prominent factors that give an indication of whether or not there exists an improvement are: the unemployment rate, domestic debt, department services such as municipalities and the social expenditures... then government debt ...These three show the movement on the labor market, and the movement on the currency trading market, as well as the movement on the markets of governmental and private projects. Therefore we will focus our research on them, and then discern the truth about the alleged improvement of the global economy.

First: The United States of America:

1. Unemployment rate :

The Central Bank has deliberately since late 2008 reduced interest rates on loans to near zero. It has doubled its balance sheet three times for up to about $3 trillion since then through the bond-buying program. In its last meeting the Central Bank has settled it at a monthly rate of $85 billion, all in order to reduce borrowing costs on the long-term, and then to facilitate the taking of loans for owners of business and projects to stimulate the labor market. However the unemployment rate continued to be high last month at 7.9 %, which is not much different from 5 years ago, when it reached 8.9 %. Although the United States approved the stimulus bill, i.e. pumping money into companies through buying shares, which began to be applied in 2009, the economy has not recovered! It did not lower the unemployment rate much ,indicating that a deep crisis is still going on, and the economy has not improved.

2. Debt of the service sector such as municipalities:

Sky News Arabia website reported on 08/11/2013 that "the burden of debt in the cities and municipalities of the United States and the inability to repay led to the bankruptcy of 41 cities within two years ,"which means that many American cities did not succeed in overcoming the effects of the global financial crisis until today. The ghost of bankruptcy returned to loom over American cities, after the State of Detroit requested to officially announce its bankruptcy last July, due to its inability to pay its debts amounting to almost $18 billion .Bankruptcy is a last resort for municipalities and cities for protection from creditors, in other words, to escape from reality and resort to the easiest solution. According to the statistics of the American Bankruptcy Institute, within the period between 2007 and 2011, America witnesses more than 40 cases of bankruptcy of cities and municipalities , with a rate of 8 cases per year. This news report shows that city bankruptcies during the last two years (between 2011 and 2013) were more than at the height of the crisis, as well as immediately before and after it .

This raises doubts concerning the statement that the U.S. economy has improved.

3. Governmental debt:

U.S. Secretary of Treasury, Jacob "Jack" Lew, on 08/26/2013 in his letter which he sent to Congress warned that "extraordinary measures that have been implemented last May to avoid the government's inability to pay its debts will expire in mid-October" and urged Congress to extend the right of the government to borrow." (Al-Quds website on .(2013/27/08 The U.S. Secretary of Treasury, Jacob "Jack" Lew, in his letter to the Congress pointed out that "the U.S. government will lose the resources required to meet its liabilities by 15th October of this year, if the ceiling of total debt of state is not raised, which now permits to the fullest extent a total debt of $ 16.7 trillion." He went on to warn, "Malfunction may occur on the financial markets and the economy will collapse in case the ceiling of the state debt is kept at the current level." He added, "The task of Congress is to protect the trust in the United States, because there is no other institution that possesses the legitimacy of raising the ceiling of the state debt) ".Russia Today website on 08/28/2013). I.e. the debt of the United States has reached the maximum limit of $16.7 trillion, however they are demanding the lifting of the debt ceiling to meet their obligations!

This is a picture of America's situation. The debt is too high and they have to resort to a lifting of the debt ceiling to pay their expenses ,address the deficit and to prevent economic collapse. This picture does not indicate that the state of the U.S. economy has improved, nor that they have emerged from the crisis.

Secondly: The European Union:

1. Unemployment Rate:

Christine Lagarde, the Director of the International Monetary Fund stated that "the unemployment rate in Spain and Greece is 27%", (Euronews web site 26/4/2013). She also stated on 2013/5/3 that: "Unemployment in the 17-nation euro area was 12 percent in February and the January figure was revised up to the same level from 11.9 percent estimated earlier, the European Union's statistics office in Luxembourg said today...The European Commission predicts unemployment rates of 12.2 percent this year and 12.1 percent in 2014."

Olli Rehn, Commission Vice-President for Economic and Monetary Affairs and the Euro said, "In view of the protracted recession, we must do whatever it takes to overcome the unemployment crisis in Europe."

Raymond Torres, Director of the International Institute for Labour Studies at the International Labour Organization said, "If nothing is done, there is a risk of a prolonged labour market recession in Europe with a lot of people moving into long-term unemployment or even dropping out of the labour market, which means that they no longer participate".

He added: "It is also important to adopt and to move to a growth strategy, especially in the eurozone," and he said the ILO favours better investment policies: "Without new credit to small enterprises) businesses) it is unthinkable to imagine a job recovery in Europe"   [Euronews 3/6/2013]

Euronews also added that "the Organization pointed out that unemployment rate has increased in nearly two-thirds of European countries since 2010. Over 30 million jobs are still needed to return employment rate to 56%, as it was in the pre-crisis level."

2. Social Expenditures:

Euronews webpage published on 30/8/2013: "The Nordic countries, which have been long famed for their generous welfare states, are counting the cost and finding they can no longer afford such entitlements for their citizens, according to Denmark's finance minister Bjarne Corydon. The Organisation for Economic Co-operation and Development recently calculated what its members spend. France tops the list devoting 33 percent of its gross domestic product on welfare. It is followed by Denmark (30.8 percent), Belgium (30.7 percent), Finland 30.5) percent) and Sweden (28.6 percent".(

All these rates are too low to fulfill all the needs of these countries' residents ...Except for Germany, whose social expenditures are acceptable to an extent... if these are the rates within the strongest spending countries, what would then be the situation of the other countries!?

3 .Debt:

Euronews webpage published on 22/7/2013 that, "The eurozone continues to sink deeper into debt in the first three months of this year irrespective of the measures taken to slow down the pace of fiscal tightening, as Greece, Italy and Portugal posted the worst while those with the lowest debt to GDP ratios are Luxembourg and Estonia." It also mentioned that, "The single currency bloc is trapped in recession, with a record high jobless rate and fragile prospects for economic recovery.

To help economic growth, European governments have decided to slow down the pace of fiscal tightening by quickly rising borrowing costs as investors worried that huge debts diminished their prospects of getting their money back".

It is worth mentioning that many of the EU countries borrowed money after they joined the EU, to the extent that borrowing exceeded the size of their economies. When the crisis reached Europe, many countries of the European Union were in a position which does not allow them to pay the debts they had prior to the crisis .Keeping in mind that Germany is the primary influencing State in the European economy, it has been able to impose austerity policies to reduce government expenditures and reduce the indebtedness of the nations, and it has worked on imposing this on the euro zone in the European Union, unlike America, which followed a policy of pumping money and increasing debt

Thus, these statements and reports indicate that the economy in Europe still suffers from the effects of the crisis and was unable to get out, remaining in a state of recession ,and therefore, it has not improved in a remarkable way.

Thirdly: China:

China's economy is a different matter, the Chinese economic analysts say that, "The increase in (economy) growth is largely dependent on the export and investment sectors, not on domestic consumption. And thus ,the general public does not deeply feel the extent of the high level of their living conditions". Its internal market is still very weak. It is therefore not a measure and does not affect the economies of other countries. It is primarily dependant on exports to U.S. markets as well as mutual investment with the United States, whether it be through China buying shares of American companies with hundreds of billions of dollars or purchasing for the U.S. Treasury bonds in an excess of a trillion dollars, as well as the American companies investing within China, also making its dollar cash reserves more than $3 trillion. China is not a leading state in the Capitalist world, but it is its follower due to it following the Capitalist way and its economic ties being with America, and it hastens to work on the implementation of the decisions led by the global Capitalist economic institutions under American influence. It can not declare itself as a Capital state, thereupon working on the leadership of the capitalist economy, because it formally and traditionally declares itself as a communist socialist state, and works to maintain this image officially for fear of losing its independent existence, and out of fear that those who lead the state ,and who embrace the Communist ideology, of losing their privileges .Thereby, the Communists and their party timidly act on applying that capitalist systems and maintaining their link to America's economy, the leader of capitalism.

For this reason, it is not expected that China abandons this policy, and hence take the lead in the capitalist world becoming the one affecting the world economy. Hence, when we address the financial crisis of capitalism that has affected the world ,we focus on America primarily, and Europe secondly, because the world that is dominated by the capitalist system is economically affected by these two: firstly by America and secondly by Europe.

Fourthly: Economies of the other countries:

The economies of the other countries whose impact on controlling world economy is low

-Japan's debt reached 245% of GDP according to IMF figures, who once again asked Japan to develop a medium-term credible budget plan in order to reduce this enormous debt, while not reducing the impact that more than 90% of it is owed to Japanese creditors.... "The Japanese government announced on 8/8/2013 its intention to cut about $85 billion of public expenditure within two years, i.e., the opposite of what is required by the Japanese stimulus pol...'

-As for Russia, it applies the Capitalist systems internally, and works on imitating the West in its application and in the establishment of economic organizations with other countries without having the ability to being creative, it therefore worked on establishing economic organizations with its affiliate countries like the European Customs Union which was established with Belarus and Kazakhstan in 2010, in stimulation of the European Customs Union... Over all, the Russian economy follows the Capitalist system, led by the West and works on following its footsteps and implementing its decisions as well as imitating capitalist countries in creating economic organizations ;Therefore Russia in this regard is not affecting the global economy, but is affected by the Western Capitalist economy more than the fact that it affects it effectively.

-As for the rest of the BRICS group (Brazil, India and South Africa), and the rest of the emerging nations (Mexico and Turkey)... they have no notable influence in the global economy. They directly follow the Western economy and are tied to the American and European financial markets. Some of them primarily depend on loans for the increase in growth like Turkey, which is not a real economy, and as such consumption increases with the people relying on borrowing, and likewise the state institutions and private institutions and companies. In some of them, like India, corruption is rampant and most of the funds are smuggled abroad. Thus the economies of these countries are unstable and not dependent on real economic resources. Brazil and South Africa have economic influence in their regions, South America and Africa, and not on the motion of the global economy .

In general one does not focus on these economies when studying the creation or removal of crises .

Fifthly: As for the numbers and data that are announced, they are sited as the economic institutions want in the states that issue this data "...

1. The growth in 2013 that the United States officially mentioned was in reality because the American government changed the way in which it measures the economy. It changed the way in which it measures growth by introducing intellectual property into the economy ,such as music production and the property rights of producing medicines and drugs… and this change lead to a 370 billion dollar increase in the economy, which represents a change (increase) representing 2.5%. Despite this, the economy of the United States is struggling to grow at a time in which its citizens have cut their spending; therefore, the reports that the recession has ended are due to the way in which statistics are published, and are artificial and not real .

2. As for the data issued by European officials, they too are not based on sustainable growth. The data that was announced is merely a preliminary estimate, and does not include all of Europe. They did not include countries that are suffering economically like Ireland and Greece. And the data issued was only an estimate compiled by the European data Agency, Eurostat, which depends on the data provided by the national statistics offices, which collects data differently, and depends greatly on surveys for its preliminary estimates of growth. These estimates are usually revised many times. The German statistics office indicates that the revisions can take place even four years after the preliminary estimates because additional data can be taken into account. Therefore ,given the statistical flaws, one cannot actually say that the situation in Europe has improved .

3. As for China, there have always been many questions and much suspicion around the data that is issued about its economy. China is a large country; with the largest area and largest population in the world. Collecting data about the performance of its economy is a very hefty undertaking…

What raises the doubts of observers is that China issued figures of annual gross domestic product (GDP) in the third week of January for the previous year, and it is extremely difficult for the Chinese government to organize an entire year's results within three weeks! This has given credibility to the idea that the Chinese data is in reality what it wants the world to know about its economy !

Sixthly: Conclusion:

The global financial crisis has not yet ended, and its repercussions are still present and are still being dealt with by pumping money as America does, or with austerity as Germany does in Europe. America pumps the amount of 85 billion dollars into the market, and gives this money to companies so that they will stay afloat, and Europe follows the policy of austerity. This is evidence that the crisis is still present and that the economy is not progressing normally without the intervention and help of the state, as if the state is the economy's ventilator. This is with the knowledge that the intervention of the state is at odds with the Capitalist system; as this system affirms ridding the market of the clutches of authority, so it does not allow the state to intervene in the market to rescue the companies and the rest of the financial institutions or to limit the movement of the market. It necessitates that there be absolute freedom, and that the market correct itself on its own, so according to the capitalist ideology intervention hinders advancement, and survival will be for the fittest, so the companies which are unable to work must fail so others can work, and only the companies able to compete remain in the market .This is how the economy advances and works freely according to the Capitalist theory which is contradicted by reality and refuted by the practices of the capitalist states. The causes of the crises and the sources of problems have not been dealt with and are inherent in the capitalist system. At every moment a setback may occur, like an ill man suffering from a chronic disease who is given reports that his health has improved due to some cause, and soon after other reports are given saying the opposite, so he is given analgesics and injections to keep him alive but he suffers from unending pains and aches …

Likewise the global economy has not improved and the crisis remains, and the problems still stand, and will stand as long as the capitalist system remains, resulting in poverty and deprivation for billions of people and the wasting of much wealth before it reaches the people ;wealth that they would have benefited from had it been distributed among them. So unhappiness and misery pervades the lives of many people, and a small number of venture capitalists account for a majority of the wealth. And because of this the crisis remains as a volcano, erupting sometimes and then calm at other times, but the inside of the volcano rages. From here we can say that there is no real solution except for Islam, which views the economic problem as the proper distribution of wealth, and enabling every single individual to benefit from it and obtaining their share, and preventing the accumulation of wealth in the pockets of certain people. Islam does not look at society by overview ,and does not decide that the individual's share is a given amount given the amount of wealth and resources, where in reality it all ends up the share of a very small class !

We ask Allah Almighty to return the rule of Islam, the Righteous Khilafah, that will spread happiness and contentment, and the sound economic life, not only for the Islamic Ummah, but will spread goodness to the four corners of the Earth, and Allah (swt) is mighty and wise.

03rd Dhul Qi'ddah 1434 AH
9 September 2013 CE

Chinese Economic Problem

Question:

On Wednesday 13/11/2013 the Chinese President Xi Jinping said that "China will step ahead with reforms to solve the economic problems but these reforms require careful planning and cannot be achieved between night and day…" This was in the end of a meeting held by the Chinese leadership starting on Saturday 9/11/2013 that lasted four days. This meeting was held after seven explosions took place on November 6, 2013 in one of the regional headquarters of the Chinese Communist Party – the ruling party in China. These explosions happened one week after a car crashed into a crowd of people and caught fire in a street close to Tiananmen Square, the great public square in Beijing that is considered the symbolic heart of the Chinese capital. And the Question: We hear that the Chinese economy is at an apex, so what does it mean when the Chinese leadership meets to find solutions to the economic problems? And is there a relationship between the explosions and the meeting of Chinese officials to study economic issues? May Allah (swt) reward you .

Answer:

1. Yes, there is a relationship, even if the government, as always, hastened to say: "the government blames what it calls Islamic extremists", to divert attention from the faltering economic situation that is pushing the Chinese people, particularly in the countryside and the midland, to misery and hardship, which will then push them to violent demonstrations to bring the state's attention to the economic suffering.

2. These incidents are considered a part of an underlying political trend that indicates that China is facing deep internal troubles, which will affect their

management of foreign policy. In 2005 China dealt with 87,000 cases of social unrest ,including general discontent, and demonstrations, and internal conflict .In 2010, 180,000 demonstrations, protests and other social incidents happened in China. In other words, the unrest is increasing...

3. The free economic zones in China (SEZs), which were the major source of the fast growth in China, were all set up in the eastern coast of China, and everything that comes out of the production lines is carried on ships and exported to the world. As a result the coastal region was linked to the international economy; and saw most of the rapid growth in China, as it also created a new generation of elite, all at the expense of the rest of China. The rest of China is still mainly agricultural ,with minimal infrastructure and its inhabitants living lives of poverty .According to the international study of the distribution of wealth carried out by the Boston Consulting Group in 2008, 0.2% of the population in China control 70% of the wealth in China. And the effect of this poor distribution is compounded by physical abuse, imprisonment ,lax labour laws, and extremely low wages, and the Chinese government's failure to heed the economic needs of most of its citizens.

4. The Chinese economic model that relies on low wages and high foreign exports is faltering now; and the international economic crisis in 2008 completely exposed this fact. A number of economic experts consider the Chinese economy to be in distress. The recipient of the Nobel Prize in economics, Paul Krugman said, "The signs are now unmistakable: China is in big trouble. We're not talking about some minor setback along the way, but something more fundamental. The country's whole way of doing business, the economic system that has driven three decades of incredible growth, has reached its limits. You could say that the Chinese model is about to hit its Great Wall, and the only question now is just how bad the crash will be." (Hitting China's Wall, Paul Krugman ,The New York Times, 18

July 2013) Stratfor also said: "Major shifts underway in the Chinese economy that Stratfor has forecast and discussed for years have now drawn the attention of the mainstream media. Many have asked when China would find itself in an economic crisis, to which we have answered that China has been there for awhile -- something not widely recognized outside China, and particularly not in the United States. A crisis can exist before it is recognized. The admission that a crisis exists is a critical moment, because this is when most others start to change their behavior in reaction to the crisis. The question we had been asking was when the Chinese economic crisis would finally become an accepted fact, thus changing the global dynamic." (The End of the Chinese Economic Miracle, Stratfor, 23 July 2013)

5. In the last ten years China has begun to progress in the capitalist approach to economic growth which means that economic growth is measured by an increase in production without considering distribution, so if production increases that means that the economy is strong and advanced even if it is all the fortune of a small group and the rest of the people live miserably… in other words concentration is on an increase in production without concentrating on fair distribution. If China continues on this communist/capitalist hybrid approach it will be afflicted with what affected the Soviet Union, which collapsed when it attempted to mix communism and capitalism, and became as a crow that tried to imitate another bird in the way it walks, and could not and ended up forgetting how it used to walk! And this is how China might become… Unless it realizes the source of its problems and solves them.

6 .China would be able to save itself from this crisis if it can transform from this hybrid economy, and stop focusing on high exports without first focusing on local demand by its people, and meeting the needs of this people. Otherwise, 948 million of the 1.3 billion of the people of China will continue to live on less than five dollars a day ,and the wealth will remain

concentrated in a small group that exploits the energy of the poor labourers, and then meeting the needs of a majority of the people is elusive, and production is controlled by a small portion of people who export production outside, so increase in production appears, but an increase in poverty in the lives of most of the people pushes them to demonstration and unrest… Zhou Xiaosheng, a distinguished professor in the Institute of Law and Sociology at Renmin University in China, explained the reality of China saying: "Do not forget that the current success of China is built on the fact that 300 million people exploit one billion low wage labourers. And the judicial system is unfair, and the unjust distribution of wealth makes the challenges greater".

7. China should not follow in the footsteps of the capitalist West and attribute all demonstrations and unrest to "Islamic extremism" instead of looking for the roots of the crisis of its hybrid economy that depends on increasing production and exporting it, so production increases in volume but poor distribution gets worse, and the number of people in poverty increases, and therefore demonstrations increase… We warn China that if it continues with this" Communocapitalist" economic policy it will follow the Soviets, and become a happening of the past…

We do not say to China to implement Islam they will thrive… and this is because this implementation requires the Islamic creed first, and it is not found with them… but we tell them to not imitate the capitalist West by focusing on increasing production without fair distribution by meeting the needs of a majority of the people that are affected by poverty .Otherwise, an increase in demonstrations is expected due to the dire economic and intellectual situation and not due to so called Islamic extremism as is promoted by the West… Speaking of Islamic extremism falls under political indictment, and it is a prelude to the serious indictment of China due to its occupation of eastern Turkistan by iron and fire, but all these deceptions and guile and attempts at changing reality will not make the Muslims forget

China's occupation of Turkistan. Indeed it will return, Allah (swt) willing, sooner or later to the Islamic Ummah .

وَلَتَعْلَمُنَّ نَبَأَهُ بَعْدَ حِينٍ

"And you will know its message after a while" [TMQ Sad: 88]

14th Muharram 1435 AH
17 November 2013

The Impact of America on India's Policy to Confront China

Question:

On 07/04/2014 the general election in India was launched, which will continue until 12/05/2014 and the results will be declared on 16/05/2014. The elections are contested by two large political blocs; the American-linked Bharatiya Janata Party (BJP) with its alliance, and the pro-British, the Congress Party, which since its return to power through winning the 2004 election, showed a sluggish relationship with the United States because of its association with Britain, and showed fear in confronting China... The question is what is the impact of America on India's policy in confronting China? And what is the relationship of that with the American Asia-Pacific Strategy and its motivation to Australia and Japan to enter into this confrontation? Will this policy be greatly affected by the type of the ruling party in India, whether the BJP or the Congress Party wins? Does India have the ability to deal with China? How is the balance of power between China and India?

Answer:

The answer to these questions will be clarified by reviewing the following points:

1. The United States is working to curb China by the surrounding countries in the Pacific region, particularly in the Eastern and Southern China Seas. So it builds various forms of alliances and partnerships and it strengthens relations with countries in the region for this purpose. This began more than a decade ago and with earnest when America realized that the policy of containment of China reached the end or the saturation level; that is, it cannot contain China more than it had. It drew closer to it by allowing it to join the WTO, it increased trade relations with it, and a U.S.-China Strategic

Dialogue became no longer sensitive as it was before... However, China did not come into the orbit of America, not even an ally according to this policy, and it has been unable to limit its ambitions to find its dominance on the East and South China Seas which is an important and vital area, rather a fateful one to it. China remained a state that maintains its integrity, coherence and independence as a major regional country working to strengthen its power, militarily and economically. Therefore, it began to exploit its economic power in some areas for political influence, and not just for profit, and is working to strengthen its influence in the region, which is contrary to the American policy or puts the American influence at risk. China has regional ambitions to dominate the region it deemed fateful, and is not sufficed by the landmass territory that its land stretches to remain confined in this territory as an economically large country only... America as well considers China's maritime area vital to it. And out of its arrogance, America is not content to be a regional state within the Americas, but it considers the whole world as its region! Therefore it rivals China in its region in order to expand the American international dominance... Thus, the policy of containment by drawing closer to China in trade relations and strategic dialogues; this policy did not make China to spin in the orbit of America, not even to become an ally in the known sense, but its regional policy became worrying to America. Thus the policy of containment became no longer effective alone, and America began to put its new plan that relates to the Asia-Pacific region, which requires the mobilization of about 60% of its naval force in the region. This is in addition to the policy of encirclement that America followed on China by occupying it with its regional issues... America has focused its efforts to mobilize countries of the region towards this policy of encirclement; the most prominent of these countries that can effectively influence in this cordon are three: India, Japan, and Australia...

2. As for India, it has a border with China of 3488 km long, and there are unresolved problems between them relating to this border. For a quarter of a century, rounds of talks have been held; the latest was the fourteenth

round of border demarcation between the two countries. Then they stopped, and the fifteenth round was not hold due to what happened on the 15/4/2013 when Chinese soldiers stormed the border with India and entered the Indian territory of the Ladakh region. They erected their tents, but then they withdrew after three weeks. This was a display operation by China, which wanted to send a message to India that China is ready to cross the border and enter a war with it as happened in October 1962, where the Chinese army launched an attack on the Arunachal Pradesh area and expelled Indian troops. After a month of this operation, Chinese forces launched a second attack on Indian lands, killing about 2,000 Indians. This issue remains unsolved and is called the "The Line of Actual Control". It is a hotly contested issue between the two countries, creating a constant tension. This is in addition to the tension caused by the problem of the Tibet region, occupied by China in 1950, which is adjacent to the Indian border. Thus, India cooperates with America in raising this problem by embracing the Buddhists of this region and their leader Dalai Lama where India has established the Central Tibetan Administration for him as a government in-exile. All these factors hardly make the tension between India and China remain calm...

3. America tried to exploit these tensions between China and India by driving India to confront China or stir up trouble between them in order to occupy China with this issue. Nonetheless, India fears facing China overland and the Chinese offensive messages on the outskirts of India reiterates this. Hence, America needed to find temptations for India to encourage it to continue aggravating China and occupying it with the border conflicts... So America held a strategic partnership with India as well as it held a nuclear cooperation agreement between them... In addition, the United States signed several economic and security agreements with India. So it concluded a defence pact in 2005 and a civil nuclear cooperation agreement in 2008. All this expands the horizon of security cooperation between them. As a result, the two countries are currently engaged in several unprecedented joint military exercises, as well as the large sales of U.S. arms to India

continues to grow... So when the Chief of Staff of the Indian Army General Deepak Kapoor stated at the end of December 2009, that, "The Indian army is preparing to fight a two-front war" (The Economic, 15/2/2010), America went on pressing Pakistan to reduce its forces on the Eastern front with India, and to focus its forces on the Western front to fight the Mujahideen who are fighting against America in Afghanistan and in the tribal areas. All this is so that India can focus on the northern front with China... America has also worked to increase trade with India, as the volume of U.S. exports to India has quickly increased in the past five compared to any other country. According to estimates by the Confederation of Indian Industry, the bilateral trade in services is likely to rise from 60 billion dollars to more than $150 billion in the next six years... However, India fears too much land conflict with China, in addition to that, the rulers of India from the Conference Party are loyal to Britain more than their loyalty to America they are unwilling to venture into a losing confrontation with China for the interests of America...!

4. Then America saw to detract the attention of India towards the East Pacific, specifically in the South China Sea and lured it by the presence of energy sources of oil and gas in this region to compete with China, and to confront within its Asia-Pacific Strategy. And so it was; India has agreed with Vietnam to off-shore drilling for oil and gas in the ocean off the disputed Spratly Islands with China. The Chinese Foreign Ministry spokesperson Liu Weimin stated after that: "We do not hope to see outside forces involved in the South China Sea dispute, and do not want to see foreign companies engaging in activities that will undermine China's sovereignty, rights and interests". (The Middle East 28/11/2011).

Earlier, the People's Daily Newspaper that speaks on behalf of the Communist Party, accused both India and Vietnam for their irresponsible confrontation attempts with China. America continued its attempts to encourage India towards direction into that area. Thus, on 22/07/2013, the U.S. Vice President Joseph Biden visited India and made remarks in

Washington before his visit; paving and tempting India to go to the east in the Pacific. He said, "...that India is increasingly looking east as a force for security and growth in Southeast Asia and beyond. To us that's welcome news." He also said, "We welcome India's engagement in the region and its efforts to develop new trade and transport links by land and by sea in the area." (IIP Digital 23/07/2013). A month earlier, i.e. on 24/06/2013, Kerry met with his Indian counterpart Shri Salman Khurshid in New Delhi where they jointly chaired the fourth round of the US-India Strategic Dialogue. They reaffirmed their shared vision on peace and stability in Asia and the Indian and Pacific Oceans, as well as they emphasized the continued support to strengthen regional communication and reaffirmed the importance of maritime security..." (IIP Digital 24/06/2013).

All of this clearly demonstrates the interest of America to push India to the East in the Pacific Ocean, specifically to the South China Sea... Nevertheless, India did not respond with the response America required during the past two years after America laid out its new plan regarding the Asia-Pacific region and pushed it towards the East. This is due to reasons related to the policy of the ruling Congress Party loyal to Britain, as well as to India's fear to confront China...

5. As for Australia, the United States began working on activating the role of Australia, which spins in its orbit, and promoting cooperation with it in the fields of economic and security to face China within the US Strategy in the Asia-Pacific region. For this purpose, U.S. officials at the highest levels, and in particular Secretary of State Hillary Clinton, Defence Secretary Leon Panetta, and former Chief of Staff Martin Dempsey have travelled to the city of Perth, Australia, for a meeting with their Australian counterparts. Clinton said on the day during the launch of the Asian American Centre at the University of Western Australia in Perth, "Australia is a gateway to the vibrant trade and energy routes that connect the Indian Ocean to the Pacific, energy resources produced in Australia are flowing through those routes to the entire world." And she said, "It is not surprising that foreign investment

is souring in Australia, including more than 100 billion dollars from the United States, because these increasingly waters are at the heart of the global economy and a key focus U.S. expanding engagement in the region, what we sometimes call our pivot to Asia". She also said, "The United States never actually left Asia, the United States is still a Pacific power, which is here to stay." She added, "The way of thinking of the United States about the Asia-Pacific and the Indo-Pacific region will be crucial to the future of the United States as well as to Australia." (IIP Digital 11/15/2012).

At this Centre, Clinton also mentioned America's view of India and what it wants from it, she said, "One of the United States strategic priorities is to support India's look East policy and to encourage New Delhi to play a greater role in Asian institutions and affairs." Furthermore she said, "The United States welcomes the joint Australia-India naval vessel exercises in the future, and is eager to work together the Indian Ocean Rim Association for Regional Cooperation which Australia will chair in 2013, and which the United States has now joined as a dialogue partner". (ibid.)

These ideas demonstrate the American way of thinking concerning the region; it wants to harness Australia as an active player in addressing China's moves in the region. It also shows that it did not achieve its objectives through India, the country neighbouring to China by land, and it wants Australia's engagement with India in the waters of the South China Sea. As Australia is closer to implement the U.S. policy than India, since it is considered a Western country that adopts capitalism, and is eager to colonize like any other Western capitalist country. Therefore it works and cooperates with America in the colonial invasions as it worked with Britain, and continues to work with them both because it spins in the orbit of these two countries...

6. As for Japan, America is working to boost its strength in Japan and give it a greater role in defending the region against China. America announced on 6/4/2014 its sending of additional missile defense ships to Japan in a statement by the US Secretary of Defense Chuck Hagel, "the United States

is planning to forward-deploy two additional AEGIS ballistic missile defense ships to Japan by 2017 and this step is a response to provocations from North Korea that threatened to carry out a new form of nuclear tests." He also warned China from abusing its great strength saying, "Great nations must not use coercion and intimidation, because this leads to conflict." He also said that he "wants to hold talks with China about its use of military power and to encourage transparency" (Reuters 6/4/2014). He pointed to what Russia did in Crimea to warn China of its similar actions in the contested islands with Japan saying:

"You cannot go around the world and redefine boundaries and violate territorial integrity and the sovereignty of nations by force, coercion or intimidation, whether it's in small islands in the Pacific, or in large nations in Europe." He also said, "Something else... that I will be talking with the Chinese about is respect for their neighbours. Coercion, intimidation is a very deadly thing that leads only to conflict." The American Secretary of Defense met last week with Defense Ministers of the South-East Asia states where he warned of the increased American concern over the South China Sea. (The same source) Japan's Kyodo News mentioned on 5/4/2014, "It is likely that the US Secretary of Defense and the Japanese Defense Minister Itsunori Onodera will discuss the issue of allowing Japan to exercise the right of self-defense by modifying the Japanese constitution. In addition Onodera will discuss the issue of transferring arms and defense equipment in his meeting with the US Secretary of Defense, and the two sides could reach an agreement to strengthen their cooperation in the area of defense equipment." This means that America wants to give Japan a role in defending the region against China to ease the burden on it and to arouse the nationalistic emotions of the Japanese who aspire to have self-power in their name and protect themselves independent of America.

7. As for the influence of American policy in the victory of the Congress Party or the Janata Party pertaining to its plan dealing with Asia – The Pacific Ocean, it no doubt has an effect, because the Congress Party is a

party that has long been loyal to the English, and it has political wit that is somewhat taken from its old lady Britain. Therefore, it is troubling to America, and at the same time it is elusive to it as Britain is. Hence it carries out some military agreements and trade relations but it disrupts some political relationships and strategic issues. For example, the Congress Party issued a statement in its election campaign, in which it won power in 2004, clarifying its stance on America, and criticizing the policy of the Janata Party that was previously in power. This is what came in the statement: "It is sad that a great country like India has declined to the level of having a relationship of adherence to the United States of America, where the government of the United States of America considers the adherence of India a given.

This has led to the BJP government being prepared to adapt to the priorities and policies of the United States of America without due consideration to India's vital foreign policy and national security interests." It is clear from this statement just how troubling it is to America. Nevertheless, it did not cut off strategic dialogue and returned to it in June 2010, which had begun in the era of President Bush in 2004. It described the Secretary of State Clinton, the head of the United States delegation at the India dialogue forum, as "an indispensible partner and a trusted friend." Therefore, since the Congress Party's rise to power after the defeat of the Janata Party that is loyal to America, it has become difficult to keep India in line with the implementation of America's plan to confront China except if America puts forth great temptations as we previously mentioned.

However, India's reluctance to contend with circumstances is nothing new, it happened in the time of the Janata Party, and nevertheless the Party did not raise the issue while implementing American policy. It should be known that Britain had made the Congress Party completely loyal to them, and handed power over to it when it departed, and had not budged from it, not even partly, except for a short time from 1998 to 2004 when the Janata Party loyal to America won, and then the Congress Party won in the elections of 2004-2009.

As for the current elections, which began on 07/04/2014, the results are to be announced on 16/05/2014. It was reported by various pollsters that their results indicate that the BJP and its allies are expected to win in this election, if the expectations of public opinion are true, and the electoral opinion monitoring institutions in India, and Janata wins, whether by a majority to form a government alone. And that is unlikely to some extent, or the results were significant for it to impose conditions on any government formed, if so, the policy of America to harass China through India will be possible more than the time of the Congress party rule, but it also makes it easier to implement the policy as was the case during the reign of the Janata Party, loyal to America, it breathed a sigh of relief at the time after the Congress Party ruled for decades before that. When the Congress Party came to power in 2004 they began a policy to distort the American policy in India, but the Congress Party was dodging America to achieve advantageous agreements with it before took steps to help America in its policy.

8. When comparing between China and India, China is advantaged in many ways:

China although it does not carry its ideology and waives it in its foreign, economic and financial policy, as well as waiving it in many areas of life. Except it maintains it in its ruling by the Communist Party name only to maintain the interests of the party and that of its followers and for the cohesion of the state and its independence. All of this enabled it to move independently and developed resistance from becoming a subordinate state or an orbit state that revolves in the orbit of a major country. It became a state that aspires to become a major power in the world. Liu Mengo, a Chinese colonel, professor at the National Defence University, who trains young officers, expressed it in his book, which he called "the Chinese dream". He called his country China to develop the strongest armies in the world, and to move quickly to overthrow the hero of the world, America.

He invited them to give up humility with respect to the global objectives and to jump, in order to become number one in the world. He said if China is incapable of being number one in the world in the twenty-first century and being a super power in the world, it will inevitably become marginalized... China possesses a sense of strength and challenge, and if China's objective is not limited only to maintain its territory, and accept to confront America only as a response to the movements of America towards its territory, China does not venture out to challenge America in their respective areas of influence... and if it did not begin to adopt capitalism in many areas, particularly in economy... it would have had a loud voice internationally, and its impact on the interests of America's would be most powerful. China in any case has a strong sense of force, and is working to maintain its region's self-sovereignty, even if in its own territory.

As for India, it holds no ideology and does not have ideas emanating from an ideology even though capitalism is implemented to ensure their subordination to the West, especially Britain and not for its revival and making it an independent state. It is like the other countries in the region that have capitalism imposed on it through the force of colonial power, and is still imposed by force. That is why they are not rushing to become independent and have no motivation to work strongly, swiftly, and self-consciously and self-direction. It remains a subordinate state; its policy is not independent, and it is noted that it is moving slowly in the political arena which is always under the influence and neither influential nor initiative and it is under the influence of either Britain or its first master America, which wraps its arms around it and there it established a strong political force for it. That is why it is different from China in this regard, intellectually backward, and are undisciplined by any specific intellectual basis, and those working in the political field are not disciplined by any basis therefore financial and political corruption is rife and moves to include all the politicians. It is difficult to become a major international or even a regional power, and the most it can become in the future is an orbit state orbiting other major country, whether America or Britain or both.

This is in political terms, but in economic terms, China's economy is four times India's economy. While China has been able to reduce the level of poverty in the country, the 66% of the world's poor are from India. India cannot compete with China economically. China has developed a large industrial sector, which led to the possession of large cash reserves that allowed it to affect the global economy. Manufacturing in India is still far from the level of China in terms of the production, processing, and in particular, heavy machinery and modern technology, this does not mean that India is free of these things, but they are lagging behind the level of China...

As for the military aspect, China's official military budget amounts to $119 billion representing more than three times the defence budget in India which amounts to 38 billion dollars. China has made significant progress in modernizing its armed forces, they are now creating their own storage (massive warehouses for military equipment industry such as ships, tanks and fighter planes) and the expansion of its fleet, as its active steps to control the region. However, India has recently begun to develop their capacity to finance military modernization program which still suffers from many problems. As India is still one of the largest importers of military equipment in the world. Despite two decades of efforts to develop its internal military capability, it failed to develop the shelves of value. Said Peter D. Wiseman, a senior researcher at the Institute for International Peace Research in Stockholm said, "I do not think that there are other countries in the world tried seriously to manufacture weapons and failed entirely, such as India." ("The biggest importer of weapons in the world, India would like to buy local", The New York Times, March 2014).

Thus, the comparison between China and India sees China outweighs India several times over...

9. In conclusion, the United States has worked to direct India towards the northern front of the conflict with China after it secured its western front with Pakistan; which pro-American rulers there offered major concessions

to India in the reign of the BJP's pro- America party. When the Congress Party returned to power, there was a decline in the work on this front, also called the Actual Line of Control because of India's fears of confrontation with China with the recent one threading it. Also because this party which is loyal to the British which does not encourage it to follow in the American outline. America directed India to what it calls the trend towards East or towards the Pacific region and specifically towards the South China Sea and tempted it with the presence of energy sources of oil and gas there and convinced it that it has the right from its share, and made it cooperate with Vietnam that claim it is also entitled to take a share and it has the dispute with China over the Spratly Islands there... The United States has also encouraged Australia towards it in an attempt to form a conglomerate of several countries to counter China... America worked to give a more active role for Japan to ease the burden off its defence. If the BJP is successful in the elections, which are currently underway and it reaches power once again, it is likely to see an increase in the activity of India with America in the East, the area of the South China Sea. As for the comparison between the strength of China and India, there is a major difference in the advantage of China that is exponential to India... and if China's objective is not limited only to maintain its territory, and accept to confront America only as a response to the movements of America towards its territory, China does not venture out to challenge America in their respective areas of influence... and if it did not begin to adopt capitalism in many areas, particularly in economy... it would have had a loud voice internationally, and its impact on the interests of America's would be most powerful.

12 Jumada II 1435 AH

12 April 2014 CE

Chinese Economic Rise

A.   China's economic rise is no coincidence but is part of a well-orchestrated strategy that began during the reign of Deng Xiaoping and was known to some as the "open door policy". After Xiaoping, his successors coined the term "China's peaceful rise". In essence, both the "open door policy" and the "China's peaceful rise" were about transforming China into an economic powerhouse, and translating its economic strength into a military capability that could defend China's economic and commercial interests. Nevertheless, both terms were intended to downplay any prospect of Beijing seeking to aggressively promote its ideology abroad or wanting confrontation with major powers most notably the United States. The terms were also meant to provide solace to China's neighbours that Beijing had no intention to expand its hegemony in the Asian Pacific region.

B.   Against this backdrop China rapidly grew its economy in two phases: a) reform in the countryside b) rural industrialization and enterprise reform. This was aided by the exploitation of cheap domestic labour, acquisition of technology from the West (advance technology was withheld) and Russia , speedy urbanisation, and an export driven industry geared towards selling cheap goods to the entire world. By and large, China based its export industry on that of Germany and Japan. Hence, during the 1980s and 1990s, China experienced phenomenal growth. From 1979 until 2010, China's average annual GDP growth was 9.91%, reaching an historical high of 15.2% in 1984. In the first decade of this century, China posted arecord GDP growth of 13% in 2007 before slowing down. It was during the last decade that China's economic might really became visible. China's GDP surpassed that of Italy in 2000, France in 2005, the United Kingdom in 2006 and that of Germany in 2007, before overtaking Japan in 2010 *(Nin-Hai Tseng, "China is richer, but most Chinese are still poor", CNN online, Feb 17, 2011).* This made China the world's second largest economy after the United

States. Some predict that China will become the world's largest economy by 2019 *("How to gracefully step aside", The Economist online Jan. 11, 2011).*

This period of prosperity even prompted some Chinese to invoke that Shengshi (the golden era) had arrived.

C.   Central to China's economic ascendency are its efforts to keep its currency the Renminbi (it is also known as the Yuan) within certain limits of the US dollar, thereby ensuring that its exports continue to be cheap and attractive to importing nations across the world. China accomplished this through a variety of means. For instance, when factory owners in China receive payments for goods exports to the US in dollars, the dollars are immediately exchanged for the Renminbi. This is because in China's domestic market the legal tender is the Renminbi, and factory owners have to pay their supplier, workers and settle domestic transactions (bills, costs etc.) in Renminbi. This increases upward pressure on the Renminbi, as demand for the currency rises and causes its value to increase in relation to the dollar. The Chinese Central Bank employs a variety of techniques to sweep away the excess Renminbi from the domestic market place. This includes domestic bonds and other financial instruments. The Central Bank also ploughs back the dollars in its possession into the US economy by purchasing US treasury bills. In this way, China is able to prevent its currency from appreciating relative to the dollar. By doing so, China has become the principal creditor nation to the US. As of May 2011, China held 26 percent of all foreign-held US Treasury securities (8% of total US public debt).

China has vehemently defended its Renminbi policy. Beijing has argued that if the Renminbi is allowed to appreciate too quickly, its exports will decline (as Chinese goods become more expensive and less competitive abroad), factories that make the goods will have to close, and millions of Chines workers will become unemployed and pose a grave threat to the stability of the country.

D.   Ironically America is China's largest trading partner and has had a significant role in fuelling the country's meteoric economic growth by granting Beijing America's Most Favoured Nation (MFN) status. The US annually renewed China's MFN status— despite the enormous imbalance in trade between the two countries— until it was made permanent in 2000. America tolerated this imbalance in trade, as it served two important objective

I.   To keep China perpetually occupied in running after and securing resources around the world to fuel its economic growth. This forced China to commit more and more resources into maintaining economic growth, at the expense of giving sufficient attention to increasing its military capabilities. America defeated the Soviet Union through arms racing and policy makers in Washington believed that China could be overcome by competing with her in economic terms.

II. To create a class of Chinese who would be smitten by American capitalism and values, and susceptible to bring democratic change to China. In other words, America was and is still looking to foment a revolution in China against the Communist Party through a middle class that is enchanted with capitalism.

In addition to this, the US thwarted China's ability to play a greater role in the region and world affairs. America kept successive Chinese governments occupied with internal and external issues located on China's periphery. Thus human rights concerns pertaining to China's treatment of the inhabitants of Tibet and Xinjiang were often used to put Beijing on the back foot. America exploited the issue of Taiwan, North Korea, and security in the Asian Pacific region to ensure that Chinese politicians are consumed with seemingly endless problems.

E.   However, America's disastrous war in Iraq and Afghanistan, together with the onset of the global economic crisis in 2008 brought sharply into focus Sino-American relations. America was no longer the Superpower it once was. The world had effectively moved on from a unipolar world in 1991 to a multi-polar world post Iraq invasion of 2003, where different major powers are competing with America for regional hegemony. One such emerging power is China. In fact some thinkers in the West believe that the balance of global power is shifting inexorably in China's favour. Recent book titles capture the mood: In the Jaws of the Dragon: America's Fate in the Coming Era of Chinese Hegemony (by Eamonn Fingleton, 2008); When China Rules the World: The End of the Western World and the Birth of a New Global Order (by Martin Jacques, 2009); The Beijing Consensus: How China's Authoritarian Model Will Dominate the Twenty-First Century (by Stefan Halper, 2010).

On the economic front it was apparent to the whole world that China's economy had weathered the financial storm better than both Europe and America. Hence, American political and economic leaders aggressively attacked Beijing's policy of keeping the Renminbi under value. They believed that this policy was hurting American prospects to revive its ailing economy and damaging America's ability to compete in the international markets. In January 2009, Mr. Geithner prior to becoming confirmed as US Treasury Secretary stated: *"President Obama — backed by the conclusions of a broad range of economists — believes that China is manipulating its currency." (Jackies Calmes,"Geithner Hints at Harder Line on China Trade", New York Times Online, Jan 22, 2009).*

Such criticisms are misplaced. Because the decline in dollar's strength has more to do with the Federal Reserve debasing the value of the dollar (through printing more dollars) than with China's Central Bank actively supporting a weaker Renminbi. Furthermore, China has recently allowed its currency to appreciate not because of American pressure but due to the fact that parts of its economy (property market) is overheating. This has also slowed China's GDP which is now a mere 8%. On the military front, the financial crisis prompted the US to reduce its military foot print. The Pentagon announced dramatic cuts, a number of weapon programmes were slashed and the US officially abandoned its policy of fighting two simultaneous wars. It is within this context that America and her allies in the Asian Pacific are more than ever conscience of China's military capabilities, especially its navy.

The weakening of America's primacy in the world gave impetus to China to flex its military muscles. For instance, in November 2007, the Chinese denied the USS Kitty Hawk carrier strike group access to Victoria Harbour in Hong Kong. In March 2009, a handful of Chinese navy ships openly harassed US surveillance ship the USNS Impeccable in the South China Sea. Additionally, China has modernised its destroyer fleet, has plans to acquire a couple of aircraft carriers and has invested heavily in building new class of conventional, nuclear attack, and ballistic submarines. According to Seth Cropsey, a former deputy undersecretary of the US Navy, China could field a submarine force larger than the US Navy's which has 75 submarines in commission, within 15 years. As China modernises its armed forces, it will become difficult for the US to defend Taiwan. According to a 2009 RAND study, by the year 2020, the US will no longer be able to defend Taiwan from a Chinese attack. In addition, to concentrating its forces on Taiwan, the Chinese navy is projecting more power in the South China Sea, China's gateway to the Indian Ocean and to the world's hydrocarbon transport route. *(Robert Kaplan, "The Geography of Chinese Power", Foreign Affairs May/June 2010).*

The US is alarmed at the rapid advancement of the Chinese armed forces and Beijing's desire to use its navy to deny American ships access to certain waterways and ports. Hence, of late America has been working to renew its security commitments with various countries in the Asian Pacific rim that includes Japan, Australia, Indonesia and South Korea. Last year, America pledged $6.4 billion worth of arms to Taiwan and on his visit to the Asian Pacific , President Obama agreed to permanently station 2,500 Marines in Australia, and to increase combat aircraft such as B-52 bombers. He also announced plans to supply 24 refurbished F-16C/D fighter aircraft to Indonesia and warned China about its belligerence in the South China Sea. He said, *"I have directed my national security team to make our presence and missions in the Asia Pacific a top priority…is absolutely vital not only for our economy but also for our national security."*

It is estimated that the trade via the South China Sea amounts to $5 trillion of which US enjoys $1.2 trillion. *(Robert Maginnis, "U.S. Declares Cold War With China", Human Events online, Nov 25 2011)*

America has also been trying to increase trade cooperation between the Asian Pacific countries by using the Trans-Pacific Strategic Economic Partnership Agreement (TTP) to entice Asian Pacific countries like Japan, South Korea, Malaysia, Australia, New Zealand, and Singapore into a stronger economic bond, and reduce the presence of Chinese goods to these countries.

Conclusion

China appears to have taken advantage of America's decline and is now more assertive in the South China Sea, and over territorial disputes with Japan and Vietnam. Away from the region, China is emboldened and more aggressive on international issues. Beijing has recently rebuffed the US and the West at the UN by vetoing the UN resolution over Syria. Whilst China's military is no match for US, it is still prepared to deny access to US naval ships to certain waterways and ports— beginning of a kind of new Monroe Doctrine for China. Meanwhile, the US is assessing China's newfound belligerence and is prepared to use all its resources to prevent China from supplanting it in the region in the coming decade. To paraphrase the political scientist John Mearsheimer, the United States, the hegemon of the Western Hemisphere, will try to prevent China from becoming the hegemon of much of the Eastern Hemisphere. This could be the signal drama of the age.

However, before China can really pose a threat to the US, it has number of internal challenges to overcome. China's economy is too export focussed and in danger of slowing down. In 2007, President Wen Jiabao, described China's economy as "unstable, unbalanced, unco-ordinated and unsustainable". Its aging population (this is a result of Mao's efforts to control China's population) which currently stands at 178 million for over 60 will double by 2030. This means that not only will work force shrink, but caring for the retired will become a major social issue. This year China's elite elect a new leadership. The Bo Xilai scandal has exposed anxieties at the top. A lot depends on how well China copes with these issues. If China handles these issues poorly, then rather witnessing an emerging power, the world may witness an imploding one.

The Sino-American relations present a huge opportunity for the future K*** State to influence change on a number of fronts. However, a lot will depend on where the Khilafah will be established.

China's primary source of energy supplies come from the Middle East and the countries of the Central Asia. This can provide the Khilafah with immense leverage to:

1.   Coerce China to open up second front with America in the Asian Pacific region. This can be done by pushing China to take back Taiwan, and

unify the Korean peninsula via North Korea. This will automatically trigger a war with the US and allow the Khilafah state to consolidate its liberation of Muslim lands.

2. Encourage China to deploy extra forces on its border with India, and threaten to invade Arunachal Pradesh and Aksai Chin. Again, this can be done to stretch Indian forces and prevent it from mobilizing its forces to attack Pakistan (assuming the country will be part of the K*****.

3. Coerce China to dump its dollar and euro holdings in return for cheap oil and gas. This will cause huge problems for both the US and Europe, and will certainly bring an end to their economic domination.

4. Force China to change its behaviour towards Muslims in Xinjiang, as well as to Muslims living in other parts of China. Incidentally, Xinjiang is the gateway to bring Islam to China. The other is Taiwan, which if occupied by the Khilafah state is like an unsinkable aircraft carrier and can be used to project the power of the Khilafah both on the mainland China, as well as on the East and South China Sea. This combined with the close proximity of Malaysia and Indonesia, will give the Khilafah paramount primacy in the Asian Pacific.

19 April 2012 CE

Chapter 4

Chinese Relationship with Islam

History of Muslims in China

«وَمَا أَرْسَلْنَاكَ إِلَّا رَحْمَةً لِّلْعَالَمِينَ»

"It was only as a mercy that We sent you [O Prophet] to all people."

[*Al- Anbiya*':107]

The message of Muhammad (saw) is to prevail all over the world. In accordance with this vision the Sahaba (ra) who ruled after him (saw) sought to expand the frontiers of the Islamic State. Seeking to complete his (saw) noble purpose by ensuring that one day it would encompass the entire world, it was Khalifah 'Uthman ibn Affan (ra) that initiated substantive contacts with China. With the Byzantine Romans defeated and the Persian Empire conquered, he dispatched a deputation to China in 29 AH (651AD). It was led by Sa'd ibn Abi Waqqas (ra), the maternal uncle of Muhammad (saw). Its mission was to invite the Chinese emperor to embrace Islam.

China's First Masjid and Muslim Settlers

The deputation built a magnificent Masjid in Canton city. This Masjid is known to this day as the "Memorial Mosque". There are some reports that Sa'd was eventually buried in China. Over the years Muslim trading activity through traders and merchant naval movements led many to settle in China. One of the first Muslim settlements in China was established in Cheng Aan Port during the era of the Tang dynasty.

It was from this time that the Muslims of China began to encounter the venom and hatred of the Chinese Kuffar. However, with the Khilafah still in place, the spirit of Jihad was strong amongst the Muslims. So such oppression was not met without the most appropriate response - fighting in the path of Allah. One of the first regular wars was waged at the Chinese border in 133AH. The Muslims were led by a great mujahid, Ziyad. They were far less in numbers but, with the help of Allah (swt), the Muslims delivered a crushing defeat on the Chinese. After this conquest, the Muslims came to command respect, power and complete control over the entire Central Asia, which is modern day Kazakhstan, Kyrgyzstan, Tajikistan, Turkmenistan and Uzbekistan. In 138 AH Khalifah al-Mansur dispatched a unit of 4000 armed Muslim troops to add to this awe.

These early victories opened the doors of China for the Muslims to spread and propagate the beauty and the truth of Islam. So the victories were consolidated, in accordance to the method of Islam. The Muslims settled in China and started establishing Mosques, schools and madrasas. In the cities, the Ulama were dominant. From the teaching in the madrasas many students gained immense knowledge. In the 1790's, according to tradition, there was as many as 30,000 Islamic students. The city of Bukhara, which was then part of China, came to be known as the "Pillar of Islam". It is this city that was blessed with a noble son, Imam al-Bukhari, one of the foremost of the Muhaditheen.

Jihad in the Face of Adversity

The early Muslim settlers in China saw all sorts of troubles and oppression. The tyrant rule of the Manchu dynasty (1644-1911) was the hardest and most brutal era administered against the Muslims. During this period five wars were waged against the Muslims: (1) The Lanchu war 1820-28; (2) The Che Kanio war 1830; (3) The Sinkiang war; 1847; (4) The Yunan war 1857; and (5) The Shansi war 1861.

This era is marked by gross Manchu animosity to Islam and Muslims. Muslims were slaughtered and mosques were razed to the ground. These Muslims were led by men, who did not just lie passively in the face of the oppression but declared Jihad against the oppressive regime of Manchu.

One of the military commanders by the name of Yaqub Beg (1820-77) liberated the whole of Turkestan and attempted to administer Islamic rules from 1867-77.

The Russians and British officials lamented this new force for Islam and spoke of a new Turkic-Chinese Muslim power rising from Central Asia, comprising of the provinces of Yunan, Szechawan, Shensi and Kansu. One British official stated, *"We really have before us grounds to summarise that this remote part of the world may at present be the scene of a great Muslim revival."*

China's modern Crusade Against Islam

Since the Communist take-over of Muslim East Turkestan (what the Communists call XingXang meaning 'New Frontier') in 1949, there has been an almost total news blackout in the region. It is like the Stalinist purges of the Soviet Union which accounted for some 20 million deaths, details are very difficult to ascertain.

Soon after the Communist take-over in 1949, the Mao government set about dividing the Muslims into nationalities so they would identify with their 'ethnic' origin and not their 'Muslim' identity. According to population statistics of 1936, the then Kuomingtang Republic of China had an estimated 48 million Muslims. After Mao's policies, the number was reported to have been reduced to 10 million. No official explanation has ever been given for this apparent disappearance of around thirty-eight million Muslims. The mass extermination and destruction of the Muslims of China clearly makes the much publicised plight the Tibetan monks or the democrats of Tiananmen Square pale into insignificance, but the West would not shed tears for Muslims.

Aside from the physical annihilation, Muslims have been subject to a constant attack on their Islamic identity. The period of the so called Cultural

Revolution (1966-76) showed openly the heathen attitudes and policies of the Communists with open and public calls for the abolition of Islamic practices. Muslims were banned from learning their written language or teaching their children Islam and many mosques were closed. A policy of ethnic (Muslim) cleansing has also been implemented since that time. Han (kafir) Chinese have been moved to settle in East Turkestan in a further attempt to make the province have a Non-Muslim majority. Back in 1949 the Han population constituted a mere 2-3% of the total population, now they represent a reported 38%.

These days, as can be seen from the riots in East Turkestan ('Xinjiang'), the resilience of the Muslims to the pagan communists has remained steadfast. The Communists realise the proud defiance of the Muslims cannot be broken, so they have adopted a policy of continued pressure on the Islamic way of life and establishing puppet 'Islamic' organisations and institutes which are supposed to represent the Muslims such as the Islamic Theological Institute and the Central Chinese Islamic Association. Both receive government funds and patronage. Amongst a number of pro-government functions they arrange the Hajj - the number of Hajjis is restricted and the selection is officially screened and controlled. Clearly, the Chinese authorities do not want news of their policy of oppression to Muslims to reach the Ummah.

The Defiance Remains

Despite the Chinese government tyranny, the Muslims of East Turkestan have remained steadfastly defiant. Young men sport neckties bearing a crescent and a star, bearing semblance to the symbols of the Uthmani Khilafah, a 'crime' that could land them in jail. In the Kanjacou area of Beijing, one Muslim was asked about his children - he said he had six. This is despite Chinese law that says Muslims of East Turkestan are only allowed two! The Muslims have an adoration of all things Islamic. The affinity the

Muslims of China have towards the Ummah and their wholesale rejection of the heathen communists shows the Chinese will never suppress the spirit of Islam in the Muslims of present day China. As one Chinese government official put it, *"It's like hacking them with a knife. They'll never forget the wound."* Nor should we forget the wound and let it be known the future Khalifah will have, Insha'Allah, an army of Mujahideen willing to fight for the cause of Islam right on China's doorstep.

7 July 2009
www.khilafah.com

www.ingramcontent.com/pod-product-compliance
Lightning Source LLC
Chambersburg PA
CBHW070140290526
45789CB00002B/566